STARTING AGAIN
WHEN YOU
FEEL LIKE
GIVING UP

Other Books by John F. Westfall

Getting Past What You'll Never Get Over
Coloring Outside the Lines
Enough is Enough: Grace for the Restless Heart

STARTING AGAIN
WHEN YOU FEEL LIKE GIVING UP

JOHN F. WESTFALL

© 2017 by John F. Westfall

Published by Revell
a division of Baker Publishing Group
PO Box 6287, Grand Rapids, MI 49516-6287
www.revellbooks.com

Spire edition published 2019
ISBN 978-0-8007-3605-7

Previously published in 2017 under the title *I Didn't Sign Up for This*

Printed in the United States of America

19   20   21   22   23   24   25   7   6   5   4   3   2   1

With gratitude this book is dedicated to
Bruce and Hazel Larson,
whose relentless encouragement and grace
helped me experience life as a great adventure
regardless of circumstances.
Among the many lessons they taught me
is that truth is a person, faith is a verb,
and relationships matter.

Contents

Acknowledgments

I am grateful for all the people whose lives in one way or another have contributed to the writing of this book. When *Getting Past What You'll Never Get Over* was published, I was surprised by the kind response of readers who wrote and shared their own stories of struggle and growth while going through hard and often unfair experiences. Their courage and faith were inspiring and gave me hope for the journey.

I am fortunate to have a collection of friends who encourage me regularly. Special thanks to Larry Stone, David Doherty, Bob Marlowe, Richard Merte, Sheila Gustafson, Chris Fulkerson, Randy Toms, Jane Knickerbocker, David Shiesser, Susie Weber, Sam Beler, Scott Tapp, John Ware, Pam Proske, David Pardee, Baron Schaaf, and John Berg.

Thanks to Lonnie Hull-DuPont, who is a brilliant editor, kind friend, gifted author, and fascinating person. Thanks for your gifts of affirmation and encouragement.

Thanks to my friends at Harbor Church in Seattle. We began in a home, moved to a pizza parlor, and grew in an old dance hall, and we know God isn't finished with us yet. You are my church family, and I'm grateful for your partnership in ministry.

Finally, I thank my family, who has hung in with me in joy and sorrow. Eileen and Damian never give up and never let me give up. Their love helps me find hope when everything's going wrong, and we have a lot of joy along the way.

1

I Didn't Sign Up for This

> An adventure is only an inconvenience rightly considered. An inconvenience is only an adventure wrongly considered.
>
> G. K. Chesterton

Where did my life go wrong? Did it just sort of meander off track until I got stuck in the proverbial mud? Or was everything going great until someone or something caused me to crash and burn? I don't know, but however I got here, I'm sure of two things: this is not the way I thought my life would be, and I didn't sign up for this.

Do you ever get to the point where you know if there is just one more setback you might lose it? I think back on times when I just wanted to pound the table in frustration because nothing seemed to work out the way I hoped. There are times in our lives when we can try to make good decisions, be responsible, take action, put things right, make amends, and choose wisely. Yet all our efforts and well-meaning intentions don't seem to make any difference.

The other night I was feeling nostalgic and I like old movies, so I started to watch *The Fugitive*. One of my favorite scenes involves a train that collides with a bus transporting prisoners and suddenly goes off the rails. First the engine, then one train car after another crashes and smashes as the train breaks apart, destroying everything in its way. In the movie, the crash lasts only a few seconds, but it seems to go on and on. Just when I think the crash can't get worse, it does, as more train cars smash into the pile of wreckage.

The film's portrayal of the train wreck got me thinking about some painful experiences that had left me feeling as if I had experienced a personal train wreck deep inside. These feelings come when, unexpectedly, our lives derail and we find ourselves in a seemingly never-ending deluge of problems, pain, and personal disasters.

In business and science, this situation is often referred to as the cascade effect. One small and seemingly insignificant thing occurs that triggers something else, which brings about still more responses until we find ourselves cascading like a waterfall toward the rocks below.

As I was eating lunch with a friend I hadn't seen in several years, I listened to him share some of the personal journey he had been on. The last time we had been together, honestly, I had been a little jealous. He was a great person. He was handsome and fit—a natural athlete with a beautiful wife and three marvelous kids. His business was thriving, giving him stock options and money that were far beyond my dreams. He had a growing faith in Jesus and was active in community and church events. To me, it seemed he had it all. What could possibly go wrong?

While I ate my Reuben sandwich, he shared some of his own cascade effect. He talked of choices that were bad, mistakes that were costly, and regrets that still haunted him. Investments that went sideways cost him a lot of the money. He told how pride caused him to drift away from his faith and how he began to pull away from people who cared for him. While the cancer diagnosis he received helped him refocus, it probably wasn't going to be enough to save his marriage, as his wife announced she didn't want to be married to him any longer.

Now he faced the reality of trying to reestablish his career, be a single parent, and battle the disease that was growing in his body. All without the love and support of the wife he hoped wouldn't leave. Suddenly, he pounded his fists on the table and exclaimed, "I don't want this! I don't want this!"

<hr>

It's easy to look back and wonder what happened to our "other" life. Where would we be today if this hadn't happened or that would have happened or if we had made a different choice along the way? Would we be better off? Would our lives be noticeably better? Perhaps. Yet ultimately, it doesn't matter.

Whether our lives are filled with celebrations or marred by regrets, our stories are still our own stories, and ultimately, they are gifts to us and from us to those with whom we choose to share them. When we choose to value only the good experiences, remember only the victories, and celebrate only the blessings, our lives end up lacking balance and depth of character.

Perhaps this is one reason the Bible encourages people to "give thanks in all circumstances" (1 Thess. 5:18). It is fairly easy for me to be thankful during the wonderful circumstances I've experienced, but it is not so easy to stay thankful during the painful, sad, and disorienting experiences. We are not told to give thanks *for* all circumstances, but we can willfully choose thankfulness not merely in difficult times but especially in difficult times.

As we begin to lay claim to all of life, owning our failures and successes, our heartbreaks and our celebrations, we can discover a new freedom that is rooted in the acceptance of our whole selves. More importantly, we can recognize that we are unique, unrepeatable miracles and that our lives, with all their ups and downs, are gifts from God that are valuable and matter very much.

In my own experience, I have found a tension at work within me. One side of me wants to appear as if I have a certain level of success, my life is fairly good, I'm surrounded by people who are respected and comfortable in their lifestyles, achievements along the way have helped me to be happy, and I pretty much have it all together. Yet the other side of me reminds me of disappointments, hurts, failures, betrayals, and insecurities that seem to know no end. I also share a common fear that I'll be found out, that people will discover I am not who I appear to be but am covering up my real self and pretending to be a better person than I really am.

I lived many years under the shadow of a great misunderstanding. I don't know how I got this idea or where it came from, but I believed that as soon as I got my life all together and was successful, the adventure would begin. I thought that when I worked through these problems and fixed those issues and resolved some conflicts and settled some trouble-some relationship struggles and met my established goals and experienced a comfortable, prosperous, trouble-free life, then the adventure would begin. Then I could step out in faith following Jesus, living abundantly, and being a good example for others all because I had everything under control and problems had been taken care of.

Do you know how long I waited to start living confi-dently, untroubled by problems and cares, following Christ in faith on a great adventure? I wasted so many years! Until one afternoon my friend Bruce Larson pointed out that if I was waiting to step out in faith until I had resolved every-thing and gotten my life fixed up and running smoothly, I would completely miss out on what God wanted to do in and through me. He helped me see that if I had everything together, I didn't need faith. I began to see that we need to let Jesus be Lord of our entire lives and trust him with our struggles and successes in order to experience life as a great adventure.

Paul, writing in 2 Corinthians 6, provides an intriguing example for us. He had started the church in Corinth and helped them through his letters as he traveled and taught in many other cities. Evidently, in his absence, some had tried to undermine his character through rumor and falsehood, to the extent that he now sought to commend himself to them and not let his ministry be discredited. Of course, what discredits a ministry more than presenting an image on the surface that is shown to be false when the reality under the surface is exposed?

He writes in verse 4, "Rather . . . we commend ourselves in every way: in great endurance; in troubles, hardships and distresses; in beatings, imprisonments and riots; in hard work, sleepless nights and hunger."

Reading this, I wonder how his examples can possibly make a good impression. I'm not sure I would be that open on a job application or a marriage proposal or any time I wanted people to like me.

But Paul keeps going in verses 6–10:

in purity, understanding, patience and kindness; in the Holy Spirit and in sincere love; in truthful speech and in the power of God; with weapons of righteousness in the right hand and in the left; through glory and dishonor, bad report and good report; genuine, yet regarded as impostors; known, yet regarded as unknown; dying, and yet we live on; beaten, and yet not killed; sorrowful, yet always rejoicing; poor, yet making many rich; having nothing, and yet possessing everything.

This passage startles me with its incredible honesty. I wonder if I have the courage to be that honest when talking about the events in my life.

Paul appears to be saying that if we are to really see his life, we need to consider all of it: difficulties and virtues all thrown together. We don't have to be ashamed or hide parts of ourselves or pretend some things aren't there. We can be confident because Christ meets us in our entirety and uses all the parts, not just the parts we would like to feature in order to show ourselves in the best light.

This feels a little radical to me as I look back to the way I was raised. For me, there was always a sense that wherever I was, whoever I was with, I probably didn't belong. This feeling was particularly strong when I went to church. It seemed to me, from my perspective as a child, that everyone was so wholesome.

My friends seemed to come from loving, normal families and have parents who were successful, peaceful, and easygoing. They went to church or synagogue, their dads went to work, and their moms were fabulous cooks. I couldn't expose the truth that my mom didn't cook very well. As a kid, I even took over the cooking for a while just because I couldn't take it anymore. I got the food money each week, and whatever was left over I got to keep for my allowance. I soon figured out that tuna noodle casserole cost less than roast beef and was more profitable for me.

I also knew that our family didn't get along very well. We weren't soft-spoken or easygoing. There were actually lots of fights in our home. Some were between one or two family members, but some escalated into big, loud, and sometimes violent brawls involving kids and parents. I guess we were encouraged to be fairly "assertive."

But then we'd go to church and on the way be warned not to say anything or do anything that might reflect poorly on our family. When we got there, we'd pile out of the car and look around at the other families, who appeared to have no problems at all. Maybe those early experiences taught me that it's better to pretend all is well and to try to appear good in order to fit in with all those people whose lives seem so much better and so much easier than my own.

Now when I read Paul's list of experiences, I'm encouraged that we don't have to pretend with each other; we can share honestly because we are loved by God regardless of who we are. Paul, writing to the church in Corinth, seems to tell them who he really is with all his giftedness and difficulties so that they can know him and accept him as a real person needing grace. Paul shares the truth of his life, letting them know he accepts the problems along with the blessings. His writing seems to indicate the bad experiences were not entirely unexpected. Possibly they weren't shocking to him, nor were they a shame for him to hide or ignore.

It appears that Paul's conversion on the road to Damascus was a trip that went completely out of his control. He began full of confidence and fury, sure of himself and his plan to stop the followers of Jesus even if it meant killing them. Then he had an experience with Jesus that stopped him in his tracks. Falling from his horse, he lay on the ground unable to see and not fully grasping the impact of his experience. He was then led into town, deeply disturbed, lost, blind, and needing the care and support of others perhaps for the first time in his life. Everything had gone wrong, and he probably had no idea how much his life would change now that the real adventure was about to begin.

Like many of us, Paul began his relationship with Jesus in a context of turmoil, pain, weakness, and shocking dependence. Why then would he assume the adventure of faith would be any different? I'm impressed that his life and ministry continued to reflect some of the same chaos and adventure as his conversion. Perhaps Paul felt free to share honestly with the church in Corinth because this adventure was exactly what he had signed up for.

⸻

I'm reminded of a couple who came to see me. It had been many years since I had officiated their wedding, and if we had taken a picture of the three of us that day, it would have been painfully obvious a lot of living had taken place between the wedding and our meeting. After a few minutes reminiscing about their wedding day, we began to share about our lives since that day.

They shared some of the experiences and life events that had shaped them so far. They longed to have children but had lost two babies midterm and were heartbroken. The wife told me of her health problems that seemed to never end. The husband had lost his job again, and they were worried about how they would survive with finances drying up much quicker than they had imagined. They were about to lose their home in foreclosure if something didn't come along soon.

Then right in the middle of our sharing, the husband looked at me with pain and frustration in his eyes and said, "You know, John, we did not sign up for this. This is definitely not the life we were expecting back on that day you married us."

In that moment, I felt so sad for them. I also felt a little guilty, thinking perhaps if I had been a better pastor I would have prepared them better to handle what lay ahead for them. At first, I didn't know how to respond, but then I went over to my file cabinet and opened it to the folders I had kept of all the marriages I had performed along with some notes from the premarital counseling. I looked through the pages in their file.

"Wait a minute, according to my notes, you committed to love, cherish, and be faithful to each other in sickness and in health, in times of plenty and in times of want, in joy and in sorrow. You *did* sign up for this!" We all started to laugh, realizing how much we don't understand about life as we make commitments.

"Are you sure that as you said your wedding vows that day you weren't really saying, 'I will love you only when I'm happy, wealthy, and well'?" Perhaps at times, we all think that in the back of our minds. Even when we do sign up for all of it, the good and bad of life, when we get the painful stuff, we don't want it. We want the pain to go away, and we might even consider giving up or just running away. This can happen in many situations, even in our relationships with God. We might start out enthusiastically committing to follow him through the ups and downs of life, living by faith and trusting him for whatever life brings. But then when difficulties surface and life is tough and painful and heartbreaking, we think, "This is not what I signed up for."

So we walk away from the Lord, believing he let us down and wasn't there for us, otherwise life would have been less painful. But I am finding that at this point when everything goes wrong, we need the Lord more, and we need to know we aren't alone in the struggles. When the worst happens, I want us to be able to say, "I did sign up for this—and the Lord has promised to be with me through it all, even to the end."

2

We Are All in This Together

> The greatest disease in the West today is not
> TB or leprosy, it is being unwanted, unloved,
> and uncared for.
>
> Mother Teresa

Contrary to what everyone may tell you, the most powerful element in the universe is not wind, fire, water, light, or even nuclear energy. The single most powerful element in the universe is acceptance. It is a gift that can transform the mundane into something extraordinary. It has the ability to disperse loneliness and pull people from shadows of isolation and shame into the light of caring and sharing. Acceptance bids us leave behind old scars of rejection in order to embrace life as it was meant to be.

In Alcoholics Anonymous, a phrase describes a common behavior. Members call it "terminal uniqueness." This occurs when a person visits an AA meeting, looks around the room at the people who have gathered and are sharing, and thinks to themselves, "This isn't a place for me. I'm not like these people. I'm out of here and I'm never coming back."

My friends in AA point out that it could be that the person thinks, "I'm not like these people. They have problems. They are a mess. I'm not as far gone as they are. I don't want to be around these people because we have nothing in common." Terminal uniqueness can also occur when, walking in, the person thinks, "I'm not like these people. I have terrible problems. I've made a mess of everything, and these people have it together and seem to be able to function way better than I do. So I'm leaving because I don't belong here with these people."

Of course, the same thing can happen everywhere in life, not just in AA meetings. I have witnessed it over and over again in social situations, workplaces, and even church. People walk in, look around, and determine the people there are not like them. Then they turn and go out the way they came in.

Kurt Vonnegut observed, "Many people need desperately to receive this message: 'I feel and think much as you do, care about many of the things you care about, although most people don't care about them. You are not alone.'"[1]

When we know we are accepted, we have a shared foundation on which to build, dream, and grow. When we realize we are all in this life together, knowing we belong, we have courage to face the future. But what happens when we discover we are no longer wanted by those we love and care about? How can we go on when acceptance is withdrawn and we realize their love no longer exists for us? I was about to find out the hard way. It's not unusual for us to experience losses that are painful from time to time. But when the bottom drops out of our world, the losses accumulate and our ability to cope is severely challenged.

||||||||||||||||||||||||||||||||

I never saw it coming. Sitting down with two friends from our church at a nearby coffee shop was something I did all the time. We sipped on lattes and chatted about our families and mutual friends. Then suddenly they looked very serious and said they had something to tell me. "Some people aren't happy about the direction you are leading the church, so as our pastor, you're done." That one short sentence sent shock waves through me at the time, and even now, thinking back, I guess I'm still in shock.

Looking back, I can see how fortunate I was to have a caring family and true friends who came around me to encourage and support me. But even they couldn't protect me from unraveling as everything seemed to go wrong. Of course, if anyone would have told me that I was about to embark on a great adventure, I would have thought them crazy.

At the time, I felt all alone, although in fact what I was going through was being experienced by people across the country. I read an article in the newspaper describing people who unsuspectingly walked into routine meetings where they were shocked to discover they were being thanked for their service and given a severance package and a box to pack up their things before being sent on their way. One such person, Joe, was in shock for weeks. After years of service as vice president of sales and acclaim for stellar production, he was set aside without regard for how his dismissal would destroy his life. He pointed out that even after two years, he still hadn't been able to find a job at the same level.

I was visiting with my friend Susie, who had been the first hire in a large Seattle tech company and had led her department through all the growth and stages of company development. That week she had been told that her position was no longer needed at the company. "Then a security guard followed me back to my office and watched while I packed up my personal items. Then he walked me down to my car." Stunned, she tried calling her husband on her cell phone as she drove out of the parking facility, only to discover they had disconnected her cell phone minutes before. With deep sadness, she looked at me and asked, "How could they treat me like that?"

Experiences such as what happened to Joe and Susie are becoming increasingly common. No one seems to care about men and women suffering through long periods without work or who are reduced to taking new jobs that pay only a fraction of their previous salaries, often without benefits. Many people find it difficult to share their personal and professional struggles. All the while stress grows, families struggle to survive financially, health problems increase, and self-esteem plummets.

But there is another dark side to this story. According to the Centers for Disease Control, between 1999 and 2010, the suicide rate for middle-aged men increased by more than 50 percent. In 2014, there were more deaths by suicide than by automobile accidents. At the same time, there have been disturbing increases in deaths from overdoses of painkillers and the chronic liver disease that excessive drinking can cause. Furthermore, between 2000 and 2010, the rate of adults applying for disability doubled.

"These trends are alarming," Paul Shoenfeld, columnist for *Everett Herald*, writes. "I have seen many people in this situation in the last five years in my office. They were discouraged, angry, and sad. Some were able to find jobs, some retired, although they didn't want to, and some fell into a disabling deep depression from which they didn't recover."[2]

Because of the reluctance of many men to discuss personal issues such as sadness, tearfulness, and a loss of interest in pleasurable experiences, often their depression isn't diagnosed. They may be more likely to drink, take drugs, become irritable or angry, have trouble sleeping, or act in erratic ways. When we sense impending problems in those close to us, it's important for us to draw near in supportive ways. While it may seem natural to pull away from them, feeling exasperated and frustrated with their behavior, doing so may only add to the sorrow they are feeling.

Being a person who has struggled with ongoing bouts of depression most of my life, I know firsthand how quickly we can be immobilized by feelings of hopelessness and despair. I also know the positive impact of being included and affirmed by those around me. We all need love, acceptance, and forgiveness. These are the antidotes for our depression, loneliness, and shame.

The apostle Paul compares our personal connectedness to the parts of a body.

> The body is not made up of one part but of many. Now if the foot should say, "Because I am not a hand, I do not belong to the body," it would not for that reason stop being part of the body. . . . The eye cannot say to the hand, "I don't need you!" And the head cannot say to the feet, "I don't need you!" . . . But God has put the body together, giving greater honor to the parts that lacked it, so that there should be no division in the body, but that its parts should

have equal concern for each other. If one part suffers, every part suffers with it; if one part is honored, every part rejoices with it. (1 Cor. 12:14–15, 21, 24–26)

We were never intended to live life on our own. Is it any wonder that loneliness has such a debilitating effect on us? Everyone is lonely at times, and chronic loneliness affects people from every walk of life, regardless of education, employment, or cultural situations. If you've ever felt so lonely that you didn't think you could make it through the night, you know that no matter how comfortable or successful a person may appear on the outside, the pain of feeling all alone and unloved can be overwhelming.

There is a big difference between alone time and heartbreaking loneliness. We all need some time alone when we can reflect, work, pray, dream, and plan. Time alone can be a valued change of pace if we are caught up in stressful or demanding activities.

Even though I'm extremely extroverted and become energized when I'm surrounded by people, sometimes I feel peopled out and I need to pull away to a quieter setting where I am by myself. Those who are more introverted gain energy and become more productive when they are able to get away from the distractions and interruptions of other people. For them, being with people can be stressful, and too much conversation wears them down.

Being an extrovert, I tend to seek out opportunities to be with others. But I struggle to take time to be intentionally alone. Eileen, my wife, is just the opposite. She loves her time to journal, read, and set her schedule based on things she wants to do. She even likes going to movies by herself, which seems unthinkable to me. When I ask her what is so great about sitting alone in a movie theater, she tells me how fabulous it is to sit wherever she wants without worrying about where someone else wants to sit. She likes eating her popcorn or hot dog in peace, and most of all, she can watch the movie she wants to see without having to negotiate with me, since I evidently have a different film in mind.

Regardless of our personal preferences and social comfort levels, we all can find ourselves feeling overwhelmed with the pain of emotional disconnection. We don't just need to have people around us. We also have to feel connected. Whether we have few if any people in our lives or we are surrounded by many others, feelings of loneliness can erode our relational confidence and turn us away from meaningful relationships.

Picture yourself waiting for people to call, write, or connect with you. It's easy for someone who doesn't understand you to make things sound so simple. "Just reach out to those around you and communicate with them. Of course they will understand, and you won't feel cut off and lonely." Although such people are well meaning and want to ease your struggle, they may not grasp the seeming impossibility of something so obvious as reaching out and communicating.

I listened as a friend described what she experienced: "Sometimes I want to talk with someone, and the phone is right beside me. All I have to do is pick it up and make the call, and I want to so badly. But it's like I'm weighed down in plaster of paris. I tell myself to stop making excuses and pick up the phone, but I don't move. I realize it's not physical. It's more like a heaviness in my emotions that is so overpowering. This may sound silly, but sometimes I'm afraid I won't even be able to breathe much less talk with someone. Finally, I give up or tell myself I'll try again later, knowing later will never come."

⁣⁣⁣⁣⁣⁣⁣⁣⁣⁣⁣⁣⁣⁣⁣⁣⁣⁣⁣⁣⁣⁣⁣⁣⁣⁣⁣⁣

Even if your life seems perfect, life isn't intended to be lived alone. In the very beginning, the Bible tells us, "The LORD God took the man and put him in the Garden of Eden to work it and take care of it.... The LORD God said, 'It is not good for the man to be alone. I will make a helper suitable for him'" (Gen. 2:15, 18). This implies that we are made to be in relationships, to be loved and to love. When we pull away from people for long periods of time, we feel not just lonely but a sense of being completely alone.

It seemed silly to watch Tom Hanks draw a face on a volleyball and name him Wilson in the movie *Castaway*. Yet over time, I grew accustomed to his friendly conversations with the imaginary friend. In the theater, there were lots of tears, showing how we came to care for Tom's character in his grief and sadness, when suddenly his closest friend and confidant was washed off the raft and swept away on the open sea. I can still hear those desperate cries: "Wilson . . . Wilson."

We don't need to be on a deserted island in a remote part of the ocean to realize it can be difficult to make friends. Moving to a new home, changing schools, even starting a new job can be a lonely time. Illness or disabilities can limit our opportunities to connect and make friends. Losses of any kind can impact us in significant ways. Whether it's losing someone we love, losing our job, or seeing our health diminish, we can find ourselves overtaken by a sense of loneliness and isolation. Such feelings of loneliness can erode our confidence and increase our insecurity, which makes it even more difficult to establish bonds of friendship.

When I felt overwhelmed by accumulating losses in my life, it seemed to me like I was a ghost. Not a friendly one like Casper nor a crazy, scary one like Beetlejuice. I simply sensed that I was no longer a person of substance, and I felt like I was invisible to the people around me who were going about their usual lives. School-aged kids and senior adults sometimes share this in common. Even though they are far apart in ages and life experiences, they sometimes find themselves sharing a common perception: they feel invisible to the outside world and like they don't matter very much.

Sometimes people can make a difference just by looking up and letting someone know, "I see you, and your life matters." That is the message Tinney Davidson has been delivering to kids walking past her house. She and her husband, Ken, began waving to the students on their way to and from school, and after her husband passed, she continued the tradition. Tinney spends much of her time sitting alone in the front room of her home, sometimes knitting hats and other items she donates to St. Joseph's General Hospital in her community of Comox, British Columbia. Perhaps she realized how young people sometimes feel insecure and insignificant, or maybe she simply wanted to cheer them up. She began with a wave and a smile. "I just liked the look of the children, and I thought if they look in, then I'll wave to them. And that's how it started." Every time a student looked her way, she waved and gave them a big smile. "I love it, and they seem to like it also. So it's been a fun few years."

The students began to wave back to Tinney, and the encounter became a regular part of their day. One Valentine's

Day they invited Tinney to come with them to the school. Not realizing what was in store, Tinney was surprised to discover she was being honored at a special school assembly. Showing their appreciation, the students presented a newly created video and valentines expressing their thanks for years of kindness demonstrated in waves and smiles.

Often small acts of kindness mean the most and remind us that we are all in this life together. "She waves to me every day as I walk to school," said one student. "And I can always count on her to be that warm smile on a dreary day." Another student added, "She's just one of those people who's like pumping everyone's attitude way up."

"I'm overwhelmed!" said Tinney through her tears.[3]

When love is expressed or demonstrated, something unexpected occurs. Both the person expressing love and the one receiving love feel valued and that their lives matter. When we feel valueless, we can lose sight of who we are in God's eyes. Sometimes we mistakenly assume that our value lies in our accomplishments or in what we can give to or do for others. While achievements and generosity are great, they are no substitute for honest expressions of love.

I learned this important lesson from a four-year-old attending our preschool. I enjoy volunteering in the preschool whenever I get the opportunity. Each child is unique, and some create special challenges. One student caught my attention because he was so difficult. Anthony was a terror on the playground. He fought with other kids, was willfully defiant to the teachers, and was a biter. He even bit me!

One day after class, his mom came to see me. She was distraught as she let me know how much her son struggled. She told me she thought he might have ADHD, obviously he had anger issues, and she was worried because he seemed to lack social skills. Sometimes she would find him crying at home because he had no friends. Then she said, "I was told to talk with you because you had ADHD and lots of problems as a child. I hoped you might understand what he's going through."

I thanked her for sharing and told her I'd try to think of something that might help Anthony, even though at the time I couldn't think of anything at all. The next week I had an idea. I decided that when I was around the kids, every time I said his name, I would add two words. So when he walked into the classroom on Friday morning, I greeted him, "Hey, here's my friend Anthony." As he was leaving at the end of the school session, I said, "See you later, Anthony, my friend."

I realized adding the words "my friend" wasn't much. But I kept it up every time I was around him. In class, on the playground, at snack time, I always added the words "my friend" when I said his name. Months went by, and I kept at it, even though there was no response from him. At the end of the school term, most of the kids graduated and went on to kindergarten, except Anthony, who returned for another year at our preschool.

I didn't let up. Every time I spoke his name, "Hey, my friend Anthony, would you pass me that toy?" there was no response. Months passed without response. Then one day in February, I was about to sit down in my office chair when I noticed a folded piece of paper lying on the seat. It was a little handwritten card. "Pastor John, be my valentine, Anthony."

The next Friday on the playground, I went up to him and said, "Anthony, my friend, thanks for the card you left on my chair. That was nice."

"What card?" he asked as he glowered.

"I was about to sit down in my chair and saw a card from you, so I just want to thank you for it."

"Did it have a little drawing on it?"

"Yes," I said, pulling it out of my pocket.

"Okay," he muttered as he turned and walked away.

Later in the morning, we were having snack time. I had made hot chocolate, and the teachers had brought carrot and celery sticks. So I was demonstrating to the kids how fun it is to plunge the sticks into the chocolate so they are more fun to eat. Just then Anthony looked over at me and asked, "Pastor John, am I your friend?"

This was the first time he had responded to me. I told him, "Yes, and we've been friends for almost two years."

"So we are friends." He thought for a minute, then asked, "Pastor John, can we be friends forever?"

"Yeah, of course," I told him.

About an hour later, there was a big disruption on the playground. A fight had broken out, and kids were yelling and crying. I went over to see what was happening, and I saw Anthony sitting all by himself at the edge of the play area crying. So I sat down next to him and asked what had happened.

"I pushed them when they said they wouldn't let me play with them because I called them stupid."

"So you called them stupid and pushed them, and they won't play with you now. Is that what happened?"

"Yeah." We sat in silence for a few minutes, then Anthony turned to me and said, "Pastor John, does this mean you're not my friend anymore?"

"No," I told him. "I'm not dead yet. I told you we'd be friends forever, and I'm not dead yet, and you aren't dead yet, so I guess we are still friends." Then he asked me what he should do, so I reminded him that he wouldn't like it if they called him stupid, so maybe he could go over and tell them he was sorry. He thought about it, said okay, and jumped up and ran off to apologize to the other kids.

I thought about the two years of calling him my friend with no response until that day. "Are we friends?" He had heard me after all.

Anthony graduated from preschool and headed off to kindergarten. A few months later, there was a knock on my door, and his mom was wanting to tell me something. She said that Anthony had gone to get his medical checkup before enrolling in kindergarten, and during the examination, the doctor had asked him several questions. One was, "Do you have friends?" Anthony had told the doctor yes. Then the doctor had asked, "Do you have a best friend?" Anthony had responded, "Yes, Pastor John is my best friend!"

His mom smiled. "I don't know what happened, but thanks for helping my son."

⸻

There is power in the gift of friendship, and inclusion helps heal shame and loneliness. It is easy to forget that we are in this life together. We often assume that there is something wrong with us, which makes us unlovable, so we pull away from people, which leads to more self-criticism, which reinforces our judgmental attitude toward ourselves.

Our adventure begins when we realize we are not alone. Acceptance fuels our adventure. It is the gift that says, "I may not be perfect. In fact, I'm flawed in many ways, but I'm lovable. And so are you."

3

I'm Not Stubborn, I Just Don't Want To

There is none so blind as those who will not listen.

Neil Gaiman

There is a fine line between bullheaded stubbornness and being a person of conviction. Most people see themselves as men and women of conviction, standing firm on the solid ground of noble principles and high standards. It is remarkably easy to spot the others who are just plain stubborn; their willful rigidity and inflexibility seem completely unwarranted.

This delicate distinction sometimes surfaces when I'm asked to give a reference for a friend or a colleague who is applying for a job. I want to present them in a most favorable way while at the same time being truthful and helpful to the future employer. Sometimes the situation doesn't end well.

I was talking on the phone about a possible candidate for a position. Legally, I had to give only the most basic information, but it was obvious the employer wanted as much background on the person as possible. We talked for a long time, and at the end of our conversation, he decided to hire my friend.

Three months later, the same person called back. Evidently, there were difficulties with the leadership style of the person he had hired and the expectations of the organization. Now he was angry at me! He accused me of lying to him about the candidate and intentionally misleading him to trick him into hiring the person.

"You never told us he was inflexible and unbending!"

I thought back to our original conversation. "I told you that he was the kind of person who, once he made a decision, wouldn't change his mind or be distracted by other opinions. And you said it was important that the candidate be a decisive leader who wouldn't flip-flop every time a new idea came along."

Then I reminded him that when he had asked about work style and team building, I had told him that the person was someone who preferred things to be done in a way that he considered best and that in order to maintain high standards he would work tirelessly to keep others from messing things up. "I remember you telling me that it would be wonderful to have someone who worked hard and kept the standards high, unlike the last person, who just let things drift until others came around and tried to accomplish things themselves."

There was silence on the phone. Then he said, "I guess I wasn't listening to what you were telling me because I wanted a strong, decisive leader who would be hands-on and accomplish things the right way. Now we have an inflexible dictator who won't listen to ideas and opinions from others and tries to do everything himself." Isn't it strange how one person's "single-minded decisiveness" is another's "inflexible dictator"?

⸻

We don't start out trying to be stubborn; it is just that when everything is going wrong, it's easy to misread situations and act or overreact because of the stress we feel. Our emotions and perceptions can become distorted, leading us to say or do things that are out of proportion for the situation. It's easy to lash out and become defensive or inflexible when we find ourselves stressed out.

When we are in a crisis and everything is going wrong, our responses can get sharper and more extreme than when we are in a more balanced time. Under pressure, our usual ways of operating might come across more intense to people around us.

Have you noticed that when things start to go wrong, our perceptions can become distorted? A simple comment or suggestion from a coworker or spouse seems like an insult or command in our minds. This can lead to our overreacting in a way that puts everyone on edge.

I could sense the tension in the body language of the person in front of me in line at McDonald's. I had no idea what they were thinking or what they were going through, but the vibe was pretty intense. When it was her turn to order, she kept changing her mind, and to his credit, the cashier stayed calm and friendly. While handing her the food tray, the cashier made one fatal mistake. "Have a nice day!" he said with a smile.

"Don't tell me what to do. You're not the boss of me!" she yelled, to the surprise of everyone in line.

After the shock wore off, I thought about painful times when I took innocent comments and overreacted without realizing what I was doing. It's easy to personalize and hear negativity that was never intended.

When I'm feeling like things are falling apart, and I'm over-whelmed or sad, I go grocery shopping. I know it seems weird, but it can actually be therapeutic for me to go up and down the aisles without anyone bugging me. Besides, it costs less than seeing a psychiatrist and I usually end up feeling better when I'm done.

The other day I was at the Safeway store, and I must have been feeling very down, gauging by my fully packed cart. I started to relax as I wandered up and down the aisles and even discovered bargain prices on stuff I never knew I wanted until I saw them on sale.

Not wanting to be the guy in the checkout line who every-one resents because I had so much to buy, I decided to be considerate of my fellow shoppers and use the self-checkout line. As I started ringing up my stuff, any good feelings I might have had began to fade away.

It started as a small irritation but soon turned into stress every time the computer generated "voice" told me what to do. Now, I realize it was just a machine talking to me, but in my mind the voice sounded like it was moving from instruc-tion straight to reprimand! "Place your items in the bagging area!" It began to sound quite condescending. It crossed my mind to inform the machine that I'm a college graduate with a master's degree and an earned doctorate, so quit treating me like I'm stupid! But I kept quiet and dutifully pressed on, ringing up the groceries.

There was a moment when I wondered if I was being filmed for some cable TV show, and perhaps this was all a big joke. I also noticed that none of the regular checkers had automated voices continually scolding them in front of customers. It didn't seem fair to me.

At last I was finished checking out and paid my $92.47. The receipt informed me that I had saved 39 percent. I began bagging my purchases and putting the bags in the cart. Then it started happening again. This time I was bombarded by mechanized scolding that was relentless and hostile . . . "Please remove items from bagging area!"

One time would have been a reasonable reminder, but it kept going and seemed to me to be growing louder. "Please remove items from bagging area . . . Please remove items from bagging area!" The more it repeated, the more scornful it sounded to me.

Have you ever tried to use those flimsy plastic bags when you are under extreme pressure? I had twelve bags plus four cartons of soda, and the little plastic bags seemed to conspire against me by not opening, or tearing at the bottom, so things fell out and I had to start over again. I thought to myself, "I'm trying as hard as I can—back off!"

You could have heard a pin drop in that grocery store. Guess it was more than just a thought. Did I really just shout at the cash register in the Safeway? Looking up, I felt like all the people around my area had stopped and were staring at me. The teenager at the register next to me smiled nervously. Embarrassed, I turned and took the walk of shame, pushing my shopping cart out to the parking lot.

When things go wrong, we are vulnerable and it's easy to misconstrue and take things personally. I think about all the times I gave advice without thinking. I hope my "constructive criticism" didn't sound like the mindless, inflexible, repetitive voice at the cash register. I'm going to start listening more carefully so I won't inadvertently make others feel stupid or incompetent with my helpful comments. Sometimes "Have a nice day" is enough.

We like to think of ourselves as reasonable people, and it may be difficult to see ourselves as others perceive us. I haven't yet met anyone who considered themselves stubborn. Don't misunderstand. I've met many stubborn people. They just didn't see it in themselves. When we don't want to do something, we find ways to get out of it that shift the focus away from us.

One of the most widely used excuses is that we don't know what to do. I confess to using this little excuse when I don't want to do something. Saying "I don't understand" or "I'm not sure what is the right thing to do in this instance" gets me off the hook because it implies I have to think about the situation a little more.

Stubborn Christians tend to use the popular excuse, "I'm not sure what God's will is for me." This gives the impression that God may be confused or perhaps has a communication problem that makes him unable to let us know what he has in mind. Most excuses shift the focus away from us and put the problem on someone else so we are free not to take responsibility for our action or lack of action.

What if there was no confusion about what to do or why to do it? Even with extraordinary clarity, there is still room for our excuses. When it came to making excuses in order to wiggle out of an important assignment, Moses was the poster child.

When he saw the burning bush and heard God clearly telling him how he would bring his people out of bondage and lead them to their new land of prosperity and blessing, Moses didn't respond with courage and faith. Instead, he brought up one excuse after another. Who am I to do this? Who are you, Lord? What will the people think? I have a disability, a speech impediment that disqualifies me. Finally, when all his questions had been answered and all his excuses had been resolved, he got to the bottom of his resistance: "Please send someone else" (Exod. 4:13).

As a kid in Sunday school, I never saw this side of Moses. He was portrayed as a strong, faithful leader who often faced impossible challenges and led the people with wisdom and courage, all of which may have been true. But he was also quick to make excuses and stubbornly resisted God's call in his life.

When Moses finally got to the point where he admitted he didn't want to go, we are told for the first time that God became angry. Perhaps he was angry because all of Moses's questions and excuses had been reasonable and had been reasonably answered. Now it was apparent that Moses was throwing out questions not to receive answers but in order to not take responsibility for his stubbornness. At last they were down to the real, core problem. Moses just didn't want to do it. That is often at the root of our own stubbornness: we just don't want to.

This may be one of the most significant clues to understanding why we find ourselves unable to move forward in our lives when everything goes wrong. If we peel away the layers of resistance, questions, problems, disabilities, and everyday struggles, we discover that the barrier that must be faced is the realization that we just don't want to.

When I was younger, I liked playing answer man and took pride in having answers that were clear, quick, practical, and biblical. But after a while, I learned my answers usually didn't matter. I discovered that even if I had brilliant answers, they wouldn't really make a difference, because the questions weren't actually the issue; they were merely a distraction or an excuse. The real issue for us, as it was for Moses so long ago, is that we just don't want to. We want what we want the way we want it, and we aren't open to anything else.

Jesus, praying in the garden before his arrest and crucifixion, was faced with a similar struggle. He expressed his resistance and admitted he did not want to go through what was ahead for him. "Take this cup from me" (Luke 22:42). Much like Moses, he expressed passionately that he didn't want to. Perhaps he considered alternatives to the brutality that awaited him. But then, unlike Moses, he surrendered. "Not my will, but yours be done" (Luke 22:42).

The surrender of power Jesus offered in the garden that night shows us a way to live beyond our control, fear, defensiveness, and excuses that have held us captive and limited our experience of life and love.

I don't think God particularly cares about our excuses. He isn't shocked when we don't want to do something. He knows our thoughts and isn't at all surprised. He may even be relieved that we've finally gotten through our layers of defensiveness to get down to the real issue, which is that we just don't want to do it. Is it surprising that so many churches are filled with people who have developed practiced passivity?

It has become easy to hear the challenges facing people throughout the world and respond, "Here am I, send someone else." Many of our mission programs are based on giving money so that someone else can go, leaving us right where we are most comfortable.

In *God in the Wasteland*, David Wells writes, "We have turned to a God that we can use, rather than a God we must obey. We've turned to a God who will fulfill our needs, rather than to a God before whom we must surrender our rights to ourselves. He is a God for us, for our satisfaction. And so, we've transformed the God of mercy into a god who is at our mercy."[1]

〰〰〰〰〰〰〰〰〰〰〰

I grew up with the misunderstanding that if we are obedient, everything will go smoothly. We may have problems now, but if we invite Christ into our lives, everything will clear up and be orderly and easy from then on. Except it wasn't. I learned that my room wasn't any cleaner and my grades weren't any better than before meeting Jesus. The girls I wanted to impress at school didn't like me any better, and I was still the last one picked for a team on the school playground. I admit it was a little disappointing to realize that after I accepted Christ I was still me.

A second misunderstanding Christians have is that God's will always results in our being liked, loved, and adored. There is no connection between doing the right things and being liked, loved, and adored. In fact, if we are doing the wrong things, we may find ourselves very well liked.

Moses might have been disappointed with the people's lack of appreciation for all he did for them. When he finally went back to Egypt and led the people from bondage to their new life, obeying the Lord and fulfilling his calling, how did the people respond? The people blamed him for ruining their lives. They sarcastically ridiculed him for dragging them away from their perfect lives only to destroy them in the wilderness. "Was it because there were no graves in Egypt that you brought us to the desert to die?" (Exod. 14:11).

A third misunderstanding is the belief that we can overcome any challenge we face if we are properly prepared. Somehow we get the idea that if we prepare well enough and anticipate what we might encounter, we will be able to solve the problems and overcome the obstacles on our own without needing help from God. But it's a lie. We will never be able to prepare ourselves for every challenge. All Moses could do was stay in relationship with God. When challenges came and he was powerless to handle them on his own, the reality was it took a miracle just to get by.

We also need to stay close to the Lord so that every day, when we feel overwhelmed, we recognize we need a miracle just to survive, because there is no other way to get through. This is what it means to walk by faith. If we could prepare for and overcome every obstacle, we wouldn't need faith.

A fourth misunderstanding is that trusting God means we never have to hit bottom. God isn't going to be the equivalent of a spiritual antidepressant. He won't keep us on a safe and secure level that protects us from highs or lows as we experience life. Sometimes we need to hit bottom in order to realize he is with us even when we go through the worst of life. Steve Hayner, former president of InterVarsity, was a wise friend to me. I remember him reminding me, "John, you'll never know that the Lord is all you need until you realize he is all you have."

Steve helped me see how my reluctance to let go of control and face my painful struggles kept me from discovering that God could be trusted in my worst times. His words took on greater significance when he was diagnosed with pancreatic cancer and died within the year. He died in the same way he lived: trusting that the Lord he knew was all he needed and all he had.

We don't need to fear hitting bottom. It is there we discover we are not alone; the Lord is right there with us. It is also the place we must be before we are willing to change.

4

Hope Comes in Unexpected Ways

A whole stack of memories never equal one little hope.

Charles M. Schulz

For many people, it's a lot easier to be hope-less than hope-full. I understand that, but I'm not giving up on hope just yet. In fact, I want to experience hope as a constant theme regardless of my circumstances. But there are times when I think I don't need hope because I'm doing well. Then other times I think hope is impossible because I'm not doing well. So the result is I miss out on hope no matter what.

Perhaps hope can seem so fragile and fleeting because we recoil and back away in fear at every opportunity to face life squarely with the eyes of faith. Wanting to avoid suffering, we settle for shallow, sterile lives. We pick the path of least resistance rather than choosing the rocky road of patient perseverance. We gladly settle for personality and lifestyle rather than character. And we even take wishful thinking over authentic hope.

There is a strong link between hope and patience. The Bible tells us, "If we hope for what we do not yet have, we wait for it patiently" (Rom. 8:25). Maybe an important prerequisite for having hope is practicing true patience.

One Sunday morning I was on my way to church with my friend Bob riding along in the car. We pulled up to a stoplight and sat at the signal for what seemed an inordinate amount of time. Looking around, I could see there was no one on the road, yet the light stayed red. I was about to run the red light when Bob asked, "What are you preaching about this morning?"

Without thinking, I blurted out, "Patience." Then I realized he had tricked me. Sitting there with a smirk on his face, he said nothing more, while I waited for the green light that never seemed to come.

································

Maybe I find it hard to be patient because I have already formed ideas about how long things should take. I expect things to happen according to my timetable, and when they don't, I feel bugged. While I'm not very good at being patient, I suspect I'm not alone in this.

The McDonald's hamburger chain was concerned recently because their profits had leveled off and growth wasn't occurring at a rate they expected. After extensive and expensive research concerning possible reasons, they drew the conclusion that profits were down because it used to take less than a minute from the time an order was placed until it was filled. Now, the drive-through orders take an average of two minutes thirty-six seconds. Some owners are experimenting with call centers hundreds of miles away to speed up the ordering process. What does this mean? Perhaps we can conclude that while people may not care about the quality of food, they are upset that it takes almost two and a half minutes to get it. Evidently, patience can become an issue that even affects McDonald's bottom line.[1]

Another reason we may find it difficult to wait is that we have strong compulsions to take charge and make something happen. Some of the people who appear to have great patience are actually just indifferent. When someone tells you to slow down and not be in such a hurry, they may be subtly advising you to stop caring so much. Patience was never intended to involve just sitting around not getting involved or caring much about anything. Just because someone lets life go by without it disturbing them doesn't mean they are patient.

I have endless patience for things I don't care about. Sometimes people come to me agitated about something I don't care about. They are quick to point out how we need to do this . . . now is the time . . . something must be done! When this happens, I listen and then advise them to take some time . . . not rush into anything . . . give the situation some thought. I may have appeared and perhaps even sounded patient, but I was simply expressing indifference, which can masquerade as patience and fool people.

|||||||||||||||||||||||||||||||

"Be still before the LORD and wait patiently for him; do not fret when people succeed in their ways, when they carry out their wicked schemes" (Ps. 37:7). Waiting patiently, as it's used in the Old Testament, means "to turn in pain." It is the same word used to refer to enduring the pain of childbirth. This is not the same as indifferently sitting back waiting for things to happen. Waiting patiently is not passive, as if lying on the beach is a demonstration of patience. Instead, waiting patiently involves caring, just as a mother cares greatly as she goes through labor pains while giving birth. The question is, What are we going to care about?

When we care about something so much that we agonize for the situation to be resolved, then we are engaged and involved and definitely not indifferent. Psalm 40 begins, "I waited patiently for the LORD; he turned to me and heard my cry" (v. 1). Then we are told that "he lifted me out of the slimy pit, out of the mud and mire" (v. 2). I can't imagine us being calmly indifferent when we are sinking in a filthy pit. We care desperately about getting help.

Keanu Reeves portrayed Shane, a football player being given a second chance, in the movie *The Replacements*. In a team meeting, their coach, played by Gene Hackman, asks the players to share something they are afraid of. After a few players talk about spiders, Shane says, "Quicksand." A teammate asks him to explain.

He describes how while he is playing everything seems to be fine, but then something goes wrong, and then something else goes wrong. You try to fight back, he explains, "but the harder you fight, the deeper you sink until you can't move, can't breathe, 'cause you're in over your head. Like quicksand."[2]

Everything starts to go wrong, and we can't pull ourselves out of the mess, because the more we try, the worse things get. I can relate. When living in West Africa as a kid, I stayed alert to the dangers of quicksand whenever I was exploring the jungle that surrounded our home. After returning to Southern California, I watched those Saturday morning Tarzan movies in which the villain would sometimes fall into quicksand, and it wasn't long before only a pith helmet was left floating on the surface. As I walked to school, I was always on the lookout for any quicksand that might be lurking in our neighborhood.

Then as an adult, I left that silly childhood anxiety behind. Until I visited Springfield, Illinois, to speak at a conference. I arrived early to play golf with the event leaders at the Rail Country Club. Evidently, there had been a drought, and some of the beautiful lakes on the course had severely receded. Of course, I hit my ball where the lake water used to be, and it landed on the cracked surface of what had been the bottom of the lake.

Ignoring my friends' warnings, I climbed over the barrier with its signs telling us to stay away and then ducked under the yellow tape with "cuidado" printed across it, warning of danger. I told them not to worry and made my way out across the almost dry lake bottom. Approaching my golf ball, I took one more step forward when suddenly my foot sank into the ooze and muck. My natural reaction was to put my weight on my other leg in order to extract the stuck foot from the mud. That made things worse. Now I was submerged up to both knees and sinking deeper every time I struggled to get myself out.

I didn't worry until I sank past my thighs. Now I was up to my waist with no way out. My friends on the shore expressed reluctance to risk their lives to save me. I guess they thought a new speaker could easily be arranged should I not survive this mess of my own creation. The crazy thing was that even though I knew struggling to get out was only pulling me in deeper, I kept trying anyway and kept sinking.

I was facing away from the people on the shore, so I didn't know what they were doing to rescue me, so when they yelled at me to lean backward as far as possible, I wasn't confident. Out of options by then, I did what they told me to do with great effort and found that they had been pushing boards out over the lake bottom to reach me. My back made contact with a board, which held me just enough for me to transfer my weight from the mud to the board. Looking a little like the creature from the black lagoon, I slowly crawled over the boards until I could finally stand up on solid ground. As the mud and muck covering my body dried, I walked back to the clubhouse minus my dignity. By then a crowd of people had gathered on the deck waiting to see the idiot who had almost sunk in the dry lake. It reminded me of a billboard I passed on the highway: "There is a reason for everything. Sometimes the reason is you are stupid and made bad choices!"

Trying to fight our way out only pulls us deeper into the miry pit. As our confidence is eroded and losses keep coming our way, of course we have good reason to be afraid. It would require a gigantic amount of denial not to fear when everything is going wrong.

When I first started to sink into the lake, I wasn't worried. After all, I assumed I was certainly capable of getting out of this mess without too much effort. But as I kept sinking deeper and deeper, I was forced to come to grips with my own helplessness. This wasn't easy, because my whole life had been built on the false assumption that I can handle anything. Helplessness was a new feeling for me.

Perhaps hopelessness takes root deep inside of us when we begin to believe we are helpless. It can be agonizing to suffer and not be able to fix things ourselves. When we simply give up in the face of adversity or when we are certain there is nothing we can do to change things, we feel hopeless.

Working with dogs, researchers conditioned the animals with electric shocks every time a buzzer sounded. Then the dogs were put into a cage that had shocks on one side while the other side was shock-free. All the dogs had to do to avoid suffering was go to the side of the cage free from electrical shocks.

The researchers were surprised when the animals didn't go to the shock-free side. Instead, the dogs simply gave up and lay on the floor while they continued to receive shock after shock. The researchers concluded that if an animal experiences long-term stress from painful experiences, they will give up and no longer try, even if they are offered a way of escape from the pain, because they have learned there is nothing they can do to stop the pain.[3]

What happened to the dogs can happen to us. As a child, I was a good reader and a fairly creative thinker. I was imaginative and had advanced verbal skills and a knack for drama and theater. But I was terrible when it came to math. Soon I discovered how to avoid math classes whenever possible and readily announced my ineptness when it came to anything mathematical.

Even with the dawning of "new math" in the school curriculum, I was a bonehead. "Billy ran to the store three blocks away in five minutes; he ran home a different way that took seven minutes and covered four blocks. How many oranges did he buy?" I couldn't do math! I told myself, "You will never be able to do math, so don't even try to learn it." I was right. My learned helplessness when it came to anything mathematical caused me to stop trying and ultimately lose all hope that I might someday change.

Learned helplessness robs people of hope and often leads to stresses that contribute to feelings of depression and anxiety. However, the very fact that we can learn to be helpless in stressful situations demonstrates that we are just as capable of learning new ways to respond to pain and disabling beliefs. When we step out in faith and establish goals for ourselves, even though some may not be fulfilled, we can rekindle hope deep within.

||||||||||||||||||||||||||||||

The first step to overcoming learned helplessness and cultivating hope is realizing that up until now we may have felt intensely hopeless and powerless to change. The truth is, change is possible. If we don't believe life can get better, we won't take any steps to improve, much less start out on a new adventure. Reeducating ourselves to realize life can change for the better opens our eyes to the unexpected reality of hope.

Hope is rooted in God's faithfulness. The main reason we can have hope is that God is committed to us and can be trusted to work in all of life to bring wholeness, healing, and ultimate victory. Even though our hope is established in God's faithfulness, this doesn't mean we are helpless to take steps that lead us forward and strengthen our faith and hope.

Hope grows within us when we begin to envision a new beginning as our adventure starts to come into focus. Other people can help us in this process. Since we are so close to our problems, pain, and patterns of behavior, it can be difficult for us to find a perspective that is healthy and not influenced by our helpless thinking. A friend or small group can help us get a fresh perspective. Sometimes it helps to imagine helping a friend who needs to get a renewed attitude and find some workable first steps to help them overcome a similar issue. If we think of the steps we might advise our friend to consider, we can begin to take those same steps forward.

We need to think big ideas and set new goals. Just making the effort to set a few new goals will help us realize we are not powerless to make changes and will help our minds begin to think in new, creative ways. Thinking big ideas helps us break free of our self-imposed limits. When everything goes wrong, one of the first casualties is big ideas. Our thinking grows smaller, our options seem fewer, and our worldview grows narrower.

Many years ago, James Collins and Jerry Porras wrote a book to help business leaders expand their ideas and focus on goals that to many people seemed unrealistic and outrageous. They encouraged people to think up a BHAG. They believed every company and perhaps every person needs a Big Hairy Audacious Goal.[4] While their ideas were intended for business enterprises, the principles have significant relevance for our own lives.

Elon Musk, CEO of Tesla, announced his BHAG back in 2011 during a *Wall Street Journal* interview. "I'll put a man on Mars in 10 Years!"[5] What seemed absurd in 2011 is beginning to appear plausible. Musk's company SpaceX is on track to do just what he said they would do.

Amazon began as an internet bookstore when founded by Jeff Bezos. It has grown to become one of the largest retail companies in the world. Bezos's BHAG is "to be Earth's most customer-centric company."[6]

Google was founded by Larry Page and Sergey Brin while they were students at Stanford. From the start, they intended "to organize the world's information and make it universally accessible and useful."[7] Its unofficial slogan was simply, "Don't be evil."

While it is important to set goals and think big ideas, I don't think it is helpful to start out with big action steps right from the start. In my book *Getting Past What You'll Never Get Over*, I encouraged using baby steps initially to build a history of small successes.[8] It's even all right to start with ridiculously small actions so that we can establish a few successes. Nothing nurtures success as much as success. Even if right now we have difficulty believing we can change, we should act as if it were true.

I recently downloaded Stephen Guise's book *Mini Habits: Smaller Habits, Bigger Results*. I was energized by his unique perspective. He had a big goal to exercise regularly and get in shape, but he needed a new strategy to help him succeed.

"On December 28," Stephen writes, "I was a sad person, sitting on my bed and wishing for the motivation star to come swoop down and energize me. The problem I had was exercise—I wanted it, but I wasn't getting it. After 10 years of trying and falling short of my fitness goals, I hoped for success, but expected the same results and I would have gotten them had I not changed fitness habit strategies. The motivation star never did come to save me, but I was able to turn my life around in the most embarrassing way possible. I didn't set out to climb every mountain in the world. I didn't resolve to transform my fitness on the top of a mountain as I beat my chest like King Kong. I decided to do a single push-up. Yeah, that's it."[9]

Stephen's strategy was brilliant because his action steps were "too small to fail." Even an action that is "stupid small" gives us hope and teaches us that we are not helpless failures.

〰〰〰〰〰〰〰〰〰〰

One of the things I like about the Bible is that it's pretty realistic. There is a certain acceptance of the fact that it is usual and even expected that we will suffer. But we act surprised when we go through difficult times. We can't believe our misfortune when bad things happen. We get all shook up and distraught when hurt comes to us, as if we think it is somehow reserved for everyone else. There is a link between our experience of hard times and the quality of perseverance.

"Perseverance [produces] character," the Bible tells us, "and character, hope" (Rom. 5:4). The very things we have endured, experienced, and overcome later become the marks of our identity. To be people of character means that we are authentic people engraved with the unique marks of our lives. Our emerging character allows us to experience unwavering hope no matter the circumstances we face.

When we expect everything to be quick, good, and pain-free, it is destabilizing to discover that suffering and pain are normal. Sometimes we try to tell ourselves we'll be more patient when there is no more pain and suffering, but realistically, we will be dead by then. Instead, we can choose to live, love, and care patiently. We can also choose not to miss out on an adventurous life marked by depth and character. Hope is unleashed in the moments when we choose to wait for the Lord even in the middle of our greatest cares.

5

Only One Thing Can Silence Fear

You know you are truly alive when you are living among lions.

Karen Blixen

Every adventure has an element of fear. I don't like thinking about fear, and I certainly don't want to be gripped by it. If only we could experience the satisfaction and thrill of adventure without dealing with the fear that lurks around every corner of our minds.

I don't know anyone who goes through life completely free from fear, but that doesn't mean we are doomed to live under the weight of its oppressive power. We can experience adventure and joy without fear controlling or diminishing our lives. From time to time, we all experience fear, but we don't have to be defined by it.

I don't know if fear is the most debilitating emotion, but it sure makes a mess wherever it goes. When we feel anxious, it is nearly impossible to face the day with hope and confidence. The deep-seated sense of trouble and foreboding keeps us guarded and watchful while we anticipate impending disaster. Sometimes when I'm feeling afraid, I wish I could get a glimpse of the situation from a bigger perspective. I can get so wrapped up in the current problems and the pressing immediacy of my anxious feelings that I'm unable to look beyond my experience to see the bigger picture.

I learned about the importance of perspective one Fourth of July. I'm starting to think there are two kinds of people in the world: those who get excited about Fourth of July parties and the rest of us. I admit to having a slight tendency toward being a party pooper on the Fourth, but this time I set my attitude aside to attend a big bash at the home of my friends Chris and Christina. I volunteered to flip burgers on their grill so I'd have a job to do and wouldn't have to get involved with the fireworks. As the party progressed, more and more people showed up, and things started to feel a little out of control to me, but I didn't worry because there were burgers to cook and food to serve.

Lighting firecrackers in a totally random and, to my way of thinking, potentially life-threatening manner agitated three big dogs whose owners were attending the party, and the dogs started to act uneasy. Christina solved the problem by putting the dogs in the house, where they would be sheltered from the noise of explosions, billowing smoke, and lots of guys running around blowing things up.

Even with my limited experience, it seemed to me the party was going well. People seemed to be having fun, and no one had lost a limb or put out an eye. Suddenly, a loud commotion caught our attention. Two of the dogs, wildly frenzied, had found a way out of the house and came running around the corner of the garage, barking, yelping, and, it seemed to me, trying to warn us that stuff was exploding in the yard, the street, and the driveway. Charging down the street, they were immediately chased by adults and children frantically calling after them in a futile attempt to calm their anxiety.

Of course, just then the third dog, a big golden lab, burst around the corner and headed in the opposite direction on the street. Most of the remaining partygoers dutifully chased after her, calling ineffectively to get her to stop running and return to the "house of exploding stuff." I remained at my post, dutifully flipping burgers, even though very few people seemed interested in what I was cooking because, after all, who can eat when dogs are terrified and running wild?

My friend Jonathan leaned over and whispered, "What we have here is failure to communicate." He went on to suggest that if the dogs had our perspective, they would not be anxious or stressed because they would understand that the explosions that seemed real and threatening to them were merely fun Fourth of July fireworks.

On the way home that night, I thought about what had happened. I realized that when I lose perspective or don't understand what is going on in my life, I can act just like the dogs. I panic, run away, and usually stir up the people around me so that they end up following along trying to get me to calm down. Fear can be so prevailing and disturbing that it causes us to feel overwhelmed to the extent that we lose perspective and surrender to its stranglehold on our emotions.

For some, fear is a passing dread that grips them, troubles them, and then disappears as quickly as it appeared. Others suffer with anxiety disorders that not only don't fade away but also grow in intensity until life seems unmanageable and even unbearable under anxiety's crushing weight.

Unlike fear, which is often directed at perceived threats and dangers, anxiety can grow even without a clear and present danger. Anxiety begins with a sense in a person's mind about what might happen. An idea begins to take shape, and an anxiety sufferer can remain fixated as they feel overwhelmed by a deluge of dread and worry. If they think something good might occur, the anxiety focuses on the possibility that it might not happen or something will keep them from enjoying the good thing they desired. Whether events are good or bad, an anxious person continues to suffer.

Being married to someone who struggled with debilitating anxiety most of her life, I've witnessed the devastating impact of uncontrollable fear and worry. I've learned how unhelpful it is to try to talk her out of her feelings. Because feelings are not logical, it is also futile to try to convince her that what she is experiencing isn't logical or rational. Using a unique blend of frustration and stupidity, I said some incredibly unhelpful things while trying to persuade Eileen not to feel what she was feeling. Now I can identify with golfer Phil Michelson, who after blowing the lead on the last hole of the US Open shouted, "I am such a stupid!"

||||||||||||||||||||||||||||||

Part of the reason fear is difficult for people to overcome is that it can be a necessary and important part of our human condition. Without fear, we would lose a significant aspect of our survival instinct. After all, fear keeps us alert to possible threats and dangers. It also triggers the fight-or-flight instinct within us to help us react to danger in appropriate ways. Without healthy levels of fear, we would fall prey to all sorts of dangers and potential calamities that loom around us. Recognizing the role of healthy fear is important. Sadly, many people with anxiety disorders feel shame and guilt, wrongly assuming they are bad for feeling this way.

Perhaps our most common response to fear is fleeing. This reaction has probably saved us more than we know. When someone senses danger, they don't need to think, strategize, or evaluate. They just go, now! This response gets a little complicated, however, because our perceptions of what might be a threat can change depending on our previous experiences. Animals as well as humans stop sensing danger as they become accustomed to the potential threat.

Maggie, our Cavalier King Charles Spaniel, must have been hurt at an early age. Unexpected noises set her on edge and get her barking and running around as if the house were on fire. Unfortunately, our home is filled with unexpected noises. When the oven is preheating and finally reaches the correct temperature, high-pitched beeps alert us that it is ready to go. When the microwave reaches the set cooking time, it beeps. Smoke alarms send signals that their batteries are running low, and doorbells, alarm clocks, and telephones make noise.

It took Maggie a couple of years to become accustomed to many of these perceived threats. She no longer goes nuts when the microwave beeps or the oven heats up or the phone rings. Even the doorbell can't rouse her from her napping. I'm happy to report that these irritating sounds no longer terrify her.

For us, the problem with adapting to situations that used to frighten us is that we become so used to the potential danger that we ignore the warnings that had once been so strong.

While there are times when fear motivates us to flee, fear can also be a trigger that makes us angry and combative, leading us to fight against our perceived threat. I learned to drive on Southern California freeways, so I have witnessed my share of road rage incidents. I also understand how almost instantaneously a driver can move from run-of-the-mill stress in traffic to fear in response to an inconsiderate action by the driver of a nearby vehicle to full-blown road rage, which often doesn't end well.

Fleeing or fighting are not our only options when we experience fear. Some people simply freeze. Freezing occurs when we feel distraught, are unable to think clearly, and become immobilized. Sometimes it is linked to a fear of making a mistake, so rather than doing the wrong thing, we freeze and don't do anything. To a freezer, no action is much preferred to wrong action.

Professional golfer Sergio Garcia went through a time in his career when he was a notorious freezer. He would stand in position to hit his shot and freeze. Time stood still while he gripped, regripped, gripped, and regripped his golf club. Broadcasters expressed mostly scornful opinions regarding his perceived bizarre behavior. Fellow golfers became agitated and didn't want to play with him in tournaments. It became a social media phenomenon to keep track of the "Sergio count," which was how many times he gripped and regripped his club before swinging.

When he finally was able to play without freezing, the golfing world gave a global sigh of relief. In a televised match soon after he stopped freezing, Jack Nicklaus walked up a fairway talking with Sergio. The nearby microphones caught part of their conversation, in which Jack sincerely thanked Sergio for no longer freezing. I think in that moment he spoke for the entire golfing community.

There is one more common reaction to fear: flopping. For example, a person who feels very shy in social situations may start to believe there is nothing they can do to overcome their fear of interacting socially. As a result, they give up and stop trying to engage socially, which leaves their shyness even more pronounced and out of their control.

Fleeing, fighting, freezing, and flopping are simply different ways we attempt to exert control over the events we fear are uncontrollable.

⁅⁅⁅⁅⁅⁅⁅⁅⁅⁅⁅⁅

Overcoming fear is not only possible but also necessary if we want to experience life with hope and confidence. Jesus says, "Do not let your hearts be troubled" (John 14:1). It is unfortunate that some people read these words and mistakenly pile guilt and shame on top of their fear. Perhaps they assume that if they were a better person, or had more faith, or hadn't made a mistake they'd be able to control their feelings. However, before we rush to judgment, we need to remember that Jesus is sharing out of his own experience. Only a few days earlier Jesus used the same word, *troubled*, when describing his feelings about his impending death. "Now my soul is troubled, and what shall I say? 'Father, save me from this hour'?" (John 12:27).

Feeling bad about feeling bad isn't helpful. We need tangible help to acknowledge our feelings without letting them hinder or control us. Later in John 14, Jesus says, "Peace I leave with you; my peace I give you. . . . Do not let your hearts be troubled and do not be afraid" (v. 27).

We are not left on our own to struggle with fear. Neither are we told to find and develop peace within ourselves. Jesus promises to give us his own peace even in the moments of our greatest fear. His peace becomes a gift that keeps on giving. It gives us perspective, courage, confidence, and hope when we need them most. And in case others don't understand, he even points out that it isn't the same peace the rest of the world is talking about.

There is probably no end to the advice and tips to help us have peace. Some of it may be helpful, but much of it is not. I've been told to "chill out," "take a chill pill," and even "chillax." I wish it were that simple. Sometimes I think about how different my life could have been if I were more of a cool, peaceful kind of guy.

I came up with a crazy idea about how we developed a misunderstanding about the whole idea of peace. And for good measure, I can even tell you who to blame for this misunderstanding. Perhaps the reason it is so difficult for us to experience peace comes down to one thing: the Eagles! Not the ones who fly around so beautifully. I mean the rock band the Eagles. They may be to blame for all our difficulty finding peace.

In the early years of the band, a young songwriter from San Diego named Jack Tempchin wrote a song called "Peaceful, Easy Feeling," which became a huge hit for the Eagles. When Jack and I were students at Crawford High School, we never imagined the ways that song would affect the world.

Years of listening to the Eagles sing Jack's song might have made us long for an easygoing life in which we aren't let down by those we care about and we can sleep out in the desert under the stars and not be intimidated by coyotes, bugs, spiders, or snakes. I wanted to experience that kind of peace. But life for me wasn't anything like a soft rock Eagles song. It was a lot tougher and way more frustrating.

Once I tried to get a peaceful, easy feeling like the song advocated by climbing into my VW Beetle, driving into the desert, and spending the night under the moon and stars. Unlike in the song, when morning came, I found myself covered with sand and bug bites and my right eye puffed up, swollen from a spider bite. Driving home, I turned off the car radio so I wouldn't be duped again by the Eagles.

The Bible has a lot to teach us about experiencing peace in our everyday lives. The word *peace* in the Bible does not refer to sitting around in a mellow state of mind listening to soft rock. Peace in the Bible refers to having the broken parts of our lives reset in a way that healing can happen.

All of us experience brokenness as we move through life, and we don't all mend in healthy ways. Resetting our brokenness is needed, but it isn't painless. Imagine breaking your arm and being rushed to the doctor's office. Picture the doctor carefully examining your painful injury, taking X-rays, then advising you to go home and listen to calming music while thinking positive thoughts until you experienced healing. Would it help you feel better if the doctor told you how much he loves his patients and sincerely wants the best for each of them, and even though he may not know anything about medicine, he will certainly hope you get better? It would be absurd to trust that doctor with your painful injury.

A good doctor will reset the broken bone. Sometimes they will even break the bone again to help it reset correctly. Then, if needed, they'll put a cast on your arm that may get incredibly uncomfortable, and you may find it difficult to do even the simplest tasks. After all that, it will take time for the healing to be complete, and the break may be painful for a long time, up to the moment it heals. You won't be getting that peaceful, easy feeling for quite a while.

I discovered this while vacationing in Hilton Head. My wife and I were driving back to our hotel after a nice pizza lunch when suddenly, a huge SUV swerved in front of us, completely smashing our cheap, tiny rental car. We were probably in shock, but I could hear Eileen gasping for air. "I can't breathe," she whispered, then added, "I don't want to die!"

Sitting in the crushed car, I managed to reach my cell phone and press 9-1-1 to ask for an ambulance. A policeman pulled up and started organizing things just as the ambulance arrived and the paramedics promptly gave their attention to helping Eileen.

Just then, the policeman turned toward me and asked, "Who called for an ambulance?"

"I did. My wife can't breathe."

"That is my decision to make! I'll decide if she needs medical attention!"

"I'm her husband," I told him, "and you are a late arriving officer. Let them do their job."

He turned away, muttering, then started directing traffic around the wreckage.

Eileen was taken to the hospital in an ambulance, and our vacation took an unexpected detour. She was treated by a marvelous physician whose name, believe it or not, was Dr. Snowman. He determined her sternum was broken in two places, and, he informed us, it would be incredibly painful for several months until it healed. When I asked how she would know it was healed, he shrugged and said, "It will no longer hurt." That made sense. She stayed in the hospital, and I went back to the Hilton hotel alone.

The next few months were not fun. I've never had a broken sternum, but I learned that sharp, stabbing pain happens when you move, lie down, get up, roll over, laugh, talk, or sneeze. But, and this was news to me, it also happens if I do any of those things. My rolling over in bed hurt her so much that she accused me of cruel torture even though I was asleep. Many mornings when I woke up, I'd find her glaring at me for something I must have done during the night.

The pain didn't gradually decrease until it was gone. Instead, it remained at the same agonizing level for almost three months. Then one morning she announced, "The pain is gone!" And it was. Dr. Snowman was right. Her sternum hurt up to the moment it stopped hurting. Then we knew it was healed.

Jesus tells his followers, "My peace I give you" (John 14:27). Understanding that the word *peace* means setting broken bones to bring healing provides a significant picture of the true peace Jesus promises. I'm encouraged when I think of Jesus lovingly addressing the broken places in my life. Through the years, I've had my share of breakage. I've experienced broken relationships, broken dreams, and even a broken heart on more than one occasion. I'm glad he doesn't tell me to just live with my damaged condition. I need him to examine me and set right the broken parts. I realize the healing will hurt and it won't happen instantly, but it will be sure.

Much has been written about the realization that when a broken bone heals, it becomes strongest at the place where it was broken. When Jesus heals us at the point of our brokenness, we mend in such a way that we become stronger in the areas where we once were weak.

iiiiiiiiiiiiiiiiiiiiiiiiiiiii

Each of us experiences fear in our own unique way. When you're with someone in the grip of fear, be careful not to say, "I know what you're feeling." There is no way we could know the depth or intensity of pain they are experiencing. However, the Bible points us to the one thing that can silence fear: "There is no fear in love. But perfect love drives out fear" (1 John 4:18). Fear is incompatible with love and loses its voice in the presence of love. In order to win a lasting victory over our fear, we must find a way to let God love us.

Love is the ultimate expression of grace, which is getting what we don't deserve. It's not merely a feeling or an attitude but grace put into action. It's coming alongside and helping someone live beyond themselves and helping them see themselves beyond what they ever thought they might be. God's love is active grace. It is not judgment, criticism, or critique. He treats us in a way that goes beyond what we deserve. Love was God's idea. "We love because he first loved us" (1 John 4:19). Since love begins with God, if we don't experience his love, we may have difficulty loving ourselves or anyone else. We may be sentimental and syrupy but not necessarily loving.

The Hallmark Channel was broadcasting Christmas movies 24/7 during the months leading up to the holiday. For those suffering from emotional diabetes, they are a quick, sugary fix. Watching a few of them is like eating a pile of candy; you feel good for a while, but it ultimately leaves you feeling a little queasy. Sentimentality is merely a cheap imitation of real love.

Some of us find it easier to love than to be loved. What makes it difficult for us to be the recipients of love? We want to control and stay in charge of our emotions, so we do loving things rather than allowing others to love us. For years, I worked at learning how to love God more, yet all the while I was hindering my ability to experience God's love for me. I found ways to avoid being loved perhaps because that would have implied I needed love.

Maybe we are reluctant to give and receive love for the simple reason love hurts. But it is this hurt that shapes us and actually helps us become more lovable. We want to love in such a way as to be free from hurt, yet without the hurts we are less lovable.

Anthony Hopkins, portraying C. S. Lewis in the movie *Shadowlands*, addresses the question, If God loves us, why do we have so much pain? He begins by mocking various misconceptions about God's love, such as God being in love with us and sending love letters with lots of x's and o's. He also dismisses the notion that God is like a kindly grandfather in heaven who doesn't care what happens as long as everyone's happy.

Then he shocks everyone by saying that God doesn't necessarily want us to be happy; rather, he wants us to be lovable. The problem, he explains, is that selfishness makes people hard to love. Because God creates us to be free, which includes the freedom to be selfish, he allows suffering that penetrates our selfishness and wakes us up to the real world, including seeing people as they really are.

"To put it another way," C. S. Lewis explains, "pain is God's megaphone to rouse a deaf world. But why must it be pain? Why can't he wake us up more gently with violins or laughter? Because the dream from which we must be wakened is the dream that all is well. That is the most dangerous illusion of them all. Self-sufficiency is the enemy of salvation."[1]

Sitting in my chair watching *Shadowlands*, I started to squirm a little. He was saying that self-sufficiency, which I'm proud to say I'm pretty good at, can actually keep us from finding God and experiencing his love. If we are self-sufficient, then we have no need of God, so we don't seek him and therefore we don't find him. "God loves us so he makes us the gift of suffering. The suffering in this world is not the failure of God's love; it is that love in action."[2]

As I listened to Lewis's speech, I was surprised at how true it was. Could it be that our suffering when everything goes wrong reminds us that all is not well and we are not well, that we need radical help from the Lord, because if we could take care of everything by ourselves, we would?

God is love, and his love is intended to be experienced in tangible ways in our lives. The descriptions of love in 1 Corinthians 13 give us a picture of who God is and how God treats us as his beloved children: being patient and kind; not envying or boasting; not being self-seeking, proud, angry, or rude; not keeping a record of wrongs; not delighting in evil; rejoicing in the truth; and protecting, trusting, hoping, and persevering.

These characteristics of God's behavior toward us have the power to shape us to love in the same ways so that these traits seep out of us and impact the people around us. Our love encourages them to demonstrate these same traits to the people in their lives.

Frankly, in my own life, it's been difficult to experience this kind of loving interaction all the time. Sometimes we miss love and its transforming power. Something goes wrong. I haven't met anyone who hasn't struggled in relationships.

|||||||||||||||||||||||||||||

Isn't it puzzling that we make such a big deal about love, yet we don't seem to know much about how to love? It's not that we lack information or motivation. After all, everyone wants to be considered loving. Perhaps we don't know what real love is, and that can make us afraid to find out. When we are afraid of love, we settle for something that resembles love but is actually different.

Psychiatrist Rollo May writes in his book *Love and Will*:

> The books which roll off the presses have techniques in love and sex, and they are best-sellers for a few weeks, but they have a hollow ring. For most people seem aware at some level, that the frantic quality with which we pursue technique is in direct proportion to the degree to which we have lost sight of the answer. It's an old and ironic habit of human beings to run faster when we've lost our way.[3]

There does seem to be an endless supply of books and internet blogs promising to help us develop better techniques for our relationships. I was wandering through a large bookstore when I noticed a big display for the bestseller *Fifty Shades of Grey*. I think it was around the time when the movie version of the book was released. People were milling around in nonchalant ways, trying to appear casual and uninterested. I glanced down at the books and suddenly broke out laughing. Someone had placed a stack of cookbooks, *Fifty Shades of Chicken*, on top of the table.

It is so easy to get caught up in the newest this or that, though we suspect it will end up being one more dead end in our never-ending search for love. Perhaps Rollo May is right. We run faster when we've lost our way. He goes on to suggest that too often we've become "schizoid," defined as out of touch, avoiding close relationships, and the inability to feel.

Schizoid sounds like a terrible condition of mental illness, but actually it is quite common. I've met many people who demonstrate incredible courage while going through horrendous setbacks and losses. I'm impressed to see them remain engaged, choosing to keep on loving and living in spite of the pain. But I also know people who haven't been able to do that. It is very common for hurting people to pull away, physically or emotionally distancing themselves in a desperate attempt to protect themselves from further hurt.

Sometimes we push people away in an attempt to hide our flaws and scars. Then we hide in addictions and self-destructive behaviors, which are futile attempts to block the pain of feeling unloved.

It is possible to fill our lives with people who are not personally connected with us but are a part of our network of relationships. We can be surrounded by any number of people with whom we have no meaningful interest, personal involvement, intimacy, or feelings. I call these "unrelationships." In these unrelationships, we keep others at a safe distance because we understand or suspect that when all is said and done, love hurts. Rather than move toward people in loving, caring ways, we cultivate unrelationships in which we can safely withhold ourselves.

I had a friend who had a habit that irritated me. When we were together, he would start to share something personal, then interrupt himself by saying, "I better keep that close to the vest." In exasperation, I'd ask, "Why did you bring it up in the first place?"

I finally realized we didn't have a real relationship because I was the only one sharing. He may have had a personal relationship with his vest, but he didn't with me. Withholding was such a habit for him that he may not have even recognized when he was doing it. By keeping everything close, we don't have to share, we don't have to connect in a meaningful way, and most of all, we don't have to hurt.

A second characteristic of unrelationships is that they are marked by our deep need to please people and our strong desire for them to please us. We replace authentic relationships with these relational barter systems based on pleasing and being pleased. We look for clues and search people's eyes in an attempt to find out what they want from us, or need from us, or what kind of person they want us to be for them, and then we try to become the person they want us to be. Meanwhile, we are actively seeking those who will please us and become who we want them to be. Such ways of relating are poor substitutes for love.

Withholding and pleasing are two ways to remain in unrelationships, but they are supported by a third characteristic: control. When our desire for control creeps into our relationships, they quickly morph into unrelationships. We may think we are helping, we may intend to improve the person, we may even believe we are right, but we are not loving. Our control issues run around wreaking havoc on people and turning loving relationships into empty shells. They are like relational zombies that must be destroyed before they destroy us.

I have to fight against my controlling tendencies every day. Without even thinking, I blurt out things like, "Not like that. The right way to do it is this way." People who know me well laugh at me when I start maneuvering and manipulating to get my way. I guess I'm not very subtle when it comes to being in control.

One Sunday morning I helped prepare the refreshments that are served at Harbor Church. People were involved cutting bagels and setting out donuts, fruit, and coffee. I helped by preparing a bowl of cream cheese to serve with the bagels. But I couldn't find the serving bowl we use every Sunday. I searched the cupboards and behind kitchen supplies, and I even went through the custodial closet, but no cream cheese bowl was I able to find.

As more people tried to help by suggesting various alternative bowls, I became more adamant about finding the "right bowl." Finally, I was passing the sink and saw it. My precious cream cheese serving bowl was on the back of the sink counter near the faucets. It was filled with brushes, sponges, soap, and various cleaning products. And I flipped out. Everyone else was probably thinking, "What's the big deal?" And they were right.

With control, we can get people to do what we want, when we want, sometimes even the way we want. But control will never result in love. When we resort to control in relationships, they turn into unrelationships very fast.

Withholding, pleasing, and controlling are all ways we can remain in unrelationships and not have to deal with authentic love and the hurt that can accompany love. But we can change. We just need to stop and say, "All right, Lord, I'm willing to hurt. Help me know you love me and give me courage to love." That is the prayer that opens the door for us to experience authentic love.

If it is true that "there is no fear in love. But perfect love drives out fear" (1 John 4:18), I want to experience this powerful love silencing my fears.

I still don't care to hurt, and I have spent many years attempting to avoid, lessen, and if possible eliminate hurt. In the process, I've probably missed out on love. I know now that if we choose to love and allow ourselves to be loved, we'll discover an important secret: we don't have to be afraid because even if love hurts, it is worth it.

6

What We Leave Behind
Makes a Difference

> We are plain quiet folk and have no use for
> adventures. Nasty disturbing uncomfortable
> things! Make you late for dinner!
>
> J. R. R. Tolkien

I've spent a total of one night in Nashville. Of course, I wanted to attend the Grand Ole Opry because I love country music. I was part of a tour group that had already visited New Orleans and Memphis, so this was the finale of our musical roots experience.

After we found our seats, my friend Pam leaned over and asked, "Have you gotten lots of good stories and ideas from our trip that you might use in your next book?"

"Nope," I blurted out before I realized she was just making small talk and didn't deserve such a blunt response.

She smiled and said, "Well, I'm going to pray that you hear something tonight that is useful." Just then the music started and the show began.

We had a great time. Even Little Jimmy Dickens came out to sing and tell a few corny jokes. No one knew this was one of his last public appearances before he died. Then Kristian Bush of the band Sugarland took the stage. Introducing his debut solo hit, "Trailer Hitch," he said, "Y'all know what they say in Tennessee?"

I turned to Pam and said, "No, I actually have no idea what they say in Tennessee."

"Well," he continued, "around here we say, 'There ain't no trailer hitch on a hearse!'"

I heard Pam whisper, "Tennessee people are very wise."

Since we already know we aren't taking stuff with us when we leave this earthly life, you'd think it would be easy to apply the same principle in our everyday lives. But it isn't always easy to let things go.

It's a good thing no one comes into my study, where I do most of my writing. They would probably sit me down and make me watch episodes of *Hoarders*. There are the usual boxes, with papers and things spilling out, on top of other boxes, with papers and things spilling out. I have a little pathway so I can (with effort and balance) get from the door to my chair and desk. Now that I think of it, the chair is the only empty, uncluttered space in the room. It swivels, so I can turn in a complete circle to see the clutter that has built up like an impenetrable fortress around me.

The old rolltop desk would be quaint if I could find it underneath the deluge of papers, books, bills, pictures, memorabilia, and unexplainable things like the clear glass vase I just noticed that is holding a Phillips screwdriver. I'd wondered what had happened to that screwdriver. It would be so easy to clear everything out so I could start anew with a clean work space. Sometimes I start to sort through things with the intent of tossing things I no longer use. But I end up just moving things from one pile or box to another pile or box, and not much is ever actually thrown away.

The same issue surfaces when I go on a trip. How much should I pack? Will I be able to haul everything around? Now that the airlines charge for checked bags, will I end up paying an exorbitant price for the privilege of carrying my burden like an out-of-shape Sherpa?

Of course, I'm not the first person in history to struggle with this problem. Jesus called the twelve disciples together in preparation for sending them out to do ministry. "He told them: 'Take nothing for the journey—no staff, no bag, no bread, no money, no extra shirt'" (Luke 9:3). Evidently, he realized they would pay so much attention to their baggage that they might miss the adventure in store for them.

Our little town of Edmonds, Washington, just north of Seattle, has a local celebrity. Rick Steves is the travel guru who developed "Through the Backdoor" travel guides. I didn't realize how famous he was until my son and I went looking for a laundromat in the south of France. Damian thought he recognized some words on a sign that indicated a laundromat. He was right, much to my relief.

While we waited for the clothes dryer to finish, the owner of the shop tried to make conversation with us by asking where we were from. Damian mentioned Seattle, and the man's face beamed with excitement. "Do you live near Mr. Rick Steves?" He seemed genuinely thrilled when Damian informed him that our home was only a couple of short blocks from Rick's office.

He invited us to crowd into his back office, where he proudly displayed a photo of himself and his wife smiling as they stood next to the famous Rick Steves. As we were leaving, I insisted on paying for our laundry, even though he kept refusing any money from such good neighbors of Mr. Rick Steves.

As we trudged back to our room, Damian and I talked about some of the travel principles that made our neighbor so well known. Like Jesus preparing his disciples for their first journey, Rick preps travelers by insisting they severely limit what they take on a trip. He sells small carry-on bags so they won't be slowed down by checked luggage. He has packing hints and cool strategies for selecting clothing to minimize options and confusion. He challenges travelers to stop worrying about what they are wearing and to shift their focus outward to notice, engage, and enjoy the people and places they visit. Evidently, he understands the importance of choosing to leave things behind as we go on our adventure.

ıııııııııııııııııııııııı

The same principles can apply to every area of our lives. We all carry baggage of one kind or another, and the sooner we unpack this baggage and leave it behind, the more freedom we will experience on our adventure. Imagine how different life would be if we took Jesus's travel advice: "Take nothing for the journey." I'd have to unpack an awful lot of baggage.

Here is a list of some emotional baggage I need to leave behind. I encourage you to make a list for yourself.

1. Guilt for the times I let people down or wasn't the person they needed me to be.

Whether we do it knowingly or unintentionally, the fact is we let people down. This is where forgiveness steps in and gives us a fresh start. Sometimes knowing we are forgiven doesn't stop us from carrying a bundle of guilt, which can result in spiritual and emotional blisters wherever or whenever the guilt rubs us the wrong way.

2. Hurts I carry with me from painful and sometimes abusive situations.

Have you been hurt? I certainly have. It is difficult to heal when we continue to pile up those painful memories and drag them behind us like dead weight. Sometimes I think I'm over something and it no longer affects me or has the power to hold me back. Then I recall the hurt and start to brood about the injustice and the unfairness as if the hurt were occurring at this very moment. I wonder, "If I let go of the hurts, will I no longer be me? Or could I become my true self by letting them go?" It's time to give them up.

3. Disappointment over things that didn't turn out the way I hoped they would.

It's possible to become so accustomed to disappointment that we expect to be disappointed. Then we aren't surprised. By holding on to our disappointment, we try to stop feeling disappointment. Of course, we also stop ourselves from feeling happy. It's like being a fan of the Chicago Cubs baseball team, who were perennial losers until a few months ago when they won the World Series for the first time since 1908. For 108 years it didn't matter the players or coaches, hitting or pitching, eventually they seemed to find a way to lose. It is easy to lose hope and accept what seems like inevitable loss. But if it can happen to the Chicago Cubs, it can happen to you and me. Why settle for a losing expectation? I want to believe this time will be different!

4. Frustrations about unhealthy choices other people made that impacted me.

Imagine how great life could be if we could make decisions for other people. When someone close to us makes the wrong (unhealthy) choice, they aren't the only ones who are affected. The negative impact touches everyone. But it's time to let go of those frustrations. They don't help us, and they weigh us down.

5. Regrets I carry from choices I didn't pursue.

"I should have . . . I could have . . . I would have . . ." We have a tendency to see the problems that resulted from decisions we made and to fantasize about how wonderful life might have been if we had chosen differently. Daydreaming about where we might be if only we had pursued the other thing is a waste of time.

6. Regrets I carry from choices I did pursue.

These regrets may be expressed with "If only . . ." and "What if . . ." When things go wrong, it is easy to speculate about how much better things might have been, but doing so doesn't allow us to move forward.

7. Sadness for hurting people with words and actions that were anything but loving.

We don't want to hurt anyone. We want to be kind and loving. Yet there were times we lashed out with words or actions that cut and wounded another person. There's no excuse, and the damage has been done. But we would love to set this sadness down and move forward as kinder people.

8. Insecurities, feelings of inadequacy, doubts, and fears about so many things.

Below the surface swirls a jumble of mixed-up feelings and insecurities that have a way of affecting nearly everything we do. These are a natural residue of the experiences and memories we've stored in our psyches. But we don't want to store them any longer. They offer no help, and they drain away our energy and creativity, which might be better used on the adventure. So good-bye to these reminders of who we've been up until now.

9. Worry that I won't have enough, be enough, or do enough for what's ahead.

Of course, we won't have, be, or do enough to meet future challenges. We don't need to. If we were capable of handling everything, we wouldn't need to trust Jesus. These concerns force us to surrender our efforts at adequacy in order to experience the power, satisfaction, and grace that the Lord wants to give us minute by minute and day by day. We should stop worrying and embrace our inadequacy so that our very adequate Lord can embrace us.

10. Finally, I want to leave behind anything that might hold me back and divert my attention away from what's important.

Even if we start small by getting rid of one thing a day, it's a start.

Eileen and I binge-watched *Downton Abbey* a while back. We started at season one/episode one and went straight through all the seasons. I soon became fascinated with the lives and intrigues of one family who was landed gentry and the people who supported their lifestyle.

One part of the series that caught my attention was the phenomenon of leaving the manor house—whether for a visit to the country, or a jaunt to London, or a journey to distant lands. All trips seemed to require a caravan of vehicles. One car carried the family members, who were followed by other vehicles transporting the help. Then following close behind were several cars and wagons piled high with stuff for the journey. The mountain of trunks, bags, and boxes seemed ridiculous and cumbersome and unnecessary. Then I saw my reflection on the television screen and thought, "That could be me hauling useless burdens wherever I go." I began to wonder if maybe I've been going the wrong way.

|||||||||||||||||||||||||||||

In addition to leaving behind emotional baggage, we need to leave our mistakes in the past. I love the scene in *Planes, Trains, and Automobiles* when, after stopping for gas in the middle of the night, John Candy sleepily drives up the highway off-ramp heading straight into oncoming traffic. A man in another car sees it happening and frantically tries to get them to turn around. "You're going the wrong way!" he yells desperately, but John Candy and Steve Martin's characters mock him and keep driving. "He doesn't know where we're going, how can he know if we're going the wrong way?" They conclude he must have been drinking, so they condescendingly wave and thank him for his misguided help, all the while ignoring the sincere warnings that they are headed for trouble. Suddenly two big rig trucks bear down on them at full speed, setting them up for a massive head-on collision and unavoidable disaster.

Why is it when we're going the wrong way, we are less able to accept help and correction when it is offered? Maybe it's because we simply don't want to be wrong. Or perhaps we don't want people to see us as wrong. Either way, my natural inclination is to ignore all the signs around me while I continue going my own wrong way.

This isn't always an easy thing to do. It's important to realize we all make mistakes but we aren't mistakes. Sometimes when we admit our mistakes, doing so opens the door to growth and new possibilities.

The Post-it notes sitting on my desk as I write this sentence were invented by a scientist who made a mistake and didn't get the stickiness of the glue right. Long before Post-it notes were discovered, Columbus set sail for Asia, and we know how that mistake turned out.

Mistakes come in all shapes and sizes. Some mistakes occur because of things we do, while other mistakes are the result of things we didn't do. Neil McCormick was an Irish teenager who was at the first practice of the band U2. Perhaps it was a mistake that he told his high school friend Bono he wasn't going to join the band because he could be more successful as a solo performer.

IBM made a big mistake turning down Bette Nesmith Graham, the bank typist who invented Liquid Paper, when she offered to sell her invention to them. When they said no, she kept selling her bottles of correction fluid, which was originally called Mistake Out, from her garage, until Gillette bought Liquid Paper for $47.5 million plus royalties.

Silly Putty was a big mistake. James Wright, an engineer working in General Electric's lab in 1943, was trying to invent synthetic rubber to aid the war effort. By mistake he made a gooey glob that scientists and the government determined had no practical use. He thought it was interesting in its stretchy, bouncy way, so he passed it around to family and friends as an oddity. That would have been the end of James Wright's big mistake if it weren't for businessman Peter Hodgson, who put it in little plastic eggs and tried without much success to sell it for a dollar. Mr. Hodgson might have wondered if he had made a big mistake until a reporter for the *New Yorker* came across it and wrote an article in the "Talk of the Town" section and orders flooded in. Silly Putty became one of the biggest-selling toys of the century.

Although he was hugely successful in his career at Decca Records, Dick Rowe will always be known for a small mistake. On the same day he auditioned the Beatles, he also auditioned Brian Poole and the Tremeloes, a band he preferred to sign. He became famous as the record company executive who turned down the Beatles with his reasoned note, "Guitar groups are on the way out."

Everyone makes mistakes. What matters is what we do with them. Mistakes can be stumbling blocks, or they can become stepping-stones toward future growth. How we choose to respond to mistakes can greatly affect our lives.

Unfortunately, we can become so upset over what happened that we follow up a mistake with actions and reactions that only make things worse. When we blame, punish, or penalize someone for their mistakes, an atmosphere of distrust and fear undermines our ability to move forward in healthy ways. If we act defensively or attempt to cover up a mistake, our actions can lead to potentially greater problems than the original mistake.

Fortunately, mistakes don't have to be the final word. They can turn into stepping-stones if we respond to them in ways that lead to healing and new opportunities.

Handling our mistakes so that they become stepping-stones is not a great mystery, nor is it difficult. When we make a mistake, our first step is to admit it. Though we may be tempted to conceal it or try to cover it up, we only delay its discovery for a little while. In the meantime, the mistake increases its negative power while it grows in the shadows of secrecy. When we accept responsibility, everyone becomes free to explore remedies and possible solutions.

Even though we know blaming others or circumstances never resolves a problem, it is almost an instinctual reaction. Perhaps it is part of our humanity, because we find it all the way back in the Garden of Eden with Adam and Eve. Not being satisfied with knowing only good, they insisted on gaining a knowledge of evil by disobeying the Lord. Their initial response was to cover up and hide. When God asked, "Where are you?" Adam's response was, "I was afraid . . . so I hid" (Gen. 3:9–10).

If Adam's first response was concealing and hiding, it didn't take long for him to shift tactics and resort to blaming and finger-pointing. In response to God's inquiry about eating from the tree, he first put the blame on Eve, then he shifted the blame back onto the Lord. "The woman *you put here with me*—she gave me some fruit from the tree, and I ate it" (Gen. 3:12, emphasis added). Not to be left out of the blame game, Eve quickly pointed her finger at the serpent.

Since the beginning of human history, this pattern of covering up, hiding, and blaming others for our mistakes has been the norm in most dysfunctional situations. Truth and health diminish when we practice plausible deniability. By accepting responsibility and handling mistakes with openness and honesty, we can move past the mistakes, learn from them, and build trust with others.

The second stepping-stone is to treat ourselves with kindness and gentleness. We need to stop beating up ourselves for making a mistake. It isn't the first one, and it won't be the last. Harshness and self-criticism wreak havoc on our hearts and minds. We need to remind ourselves that even though we made a mistake, we aren't a mistake. When we begin treating ourselves the way God treats us, with loving compassion, there is no need to punish ourselves.

The third stepping-stone is to fix the mistake, make amends if appropriate, and move on. The mistake is not the last word. It may just be a temporary setback. Mistakes can be corrected, problems fixed, and burdens lifted, and we can move forward having learned an important lesson. We don't need to hold on to the mistake or carry it around like a trophy to failure. Even Dick Rowe, the record producer who turned down the Beatles, learned from his mistake. One year later, George Harrison introduced him to an up-and-coming band, and this time, having learned his lesson, he signed The Rolling Stones.

||||||||||||||||||||||||||||

In addition to moving on from mistakes and unpacking the negative attitudes and behaviors that inhibit us from experiencing the adventure we are beginning, there is another aspect to what we leave behind. We need to consider our legacy, what we leave behind that will make a difference. Most of us won't be leaving vast amounts of money or property when we go, but we still have an opportunity to leave a legacy, one that makes an even greater impact on our world.

The shepherd's psalm, Psalm 23, is one of the most beloved parts of the Bible. I have read it at almost every funeral and memorial service I have led over the course of my life. I read it when we celebrated the lives of dear friends, church members, people with great faith, people who I wasn't sure had faith, relatives, parents, children and babies who sadly were gone too soon, and old saints who lived much longer than they wanted to.

I always read from Psalm 23 because everyone wants and needs to know that "the LORD is my shepherd, I lack nothing" (v. 1). It describes how the shepherd leads us, feeds us, nurtures us, and guides us. His strong protection allows us to "walk through the darkest valley" (v. 4) without fear of evil. I even love the part about blessing us and honoring us with a glorious banquet right in front of the people who hate us and seek our destruction. I like the image of the shepherd getting in the faces of our enemies. But it's the statement near the end of the psalm that catches my attention in a new way. "Surely your goodness and love will follow me all the days of my life" (v. 6).

As a kid growing up in Sunday school, I misunderstood this verse. I pictured myself going along living life on my own terms while goodness and love chased after me, trying to catch up with me, even though I usually stayed just out of their reach. For years, I had the idea that goodness and love were lurking out there like a couple of stalkers waiting for a chance to grab hold of me. Boy, was I wrong.

"The life I touch for good or ill will touch another life," wrote Frederick Buechner, "and that in turn another, until who knows where the trembling stops or in what far place my touch will be felt."[1] What we leave behind is a legacy of goodness and love. I think the writer of this psalm is telling us that the good we offer, the love we share, is evidence of a life well lived, and we may never see the full impact of what we do.

I met Charles at a golf club where I was warming up for an afternoon round. He walked toward me, smiled, and introduced himself, quietly letting me know that he was a member of the church where I was serving as pastor. I remember that moment we met, because it was the beginning of a growing friendship that lasted until the day he died.

I enjoyed spending time with him, asking his advice, and learning about his long and full life. He shared about his family, whom I came to know and love, and his amazing career, which culminated in his being president and CEO of one of the largest corporations in our country. Even in retirement he served on several corporate boards and encouraged a new generation of business leaders. He had a quiet, personal faith that undergirded him and kept him spiritually centered, and he was grateful for all the blessings he had experienced in his life.

Years passed, and his wife mentioned he might appreciate getting together with me. When we sat down, I could tell he was struggling. Things were different in his eyes. After a lifetime of strong, dynamic leadership in the business world, private jets, and glamorous social events, he suddenly felt like a nobody. He used to be somebody. Now he didn't know who he was. With intense sadness, he leaned forward and whispered, "Is there anything I can do that would make a difference? Nothing seems to matter anymore."

He was probably thinking I'd have some projects that could use some money he'd happily donate, but I knew that wouldn't mean anything. "Go home," I told him. "Hug your wife and thank her for standing beside you through everything, for holding your family together, and for helping you to become the man you are. Then when you're finished telling her how much you love and appreciate her, go to your daughter and let her know how proud you are of her and how much you love her. I promise you it will make a difference to them." It did. When I flew back to conduct his memorial service, they shared how his loving expressions near the end of his life had made a huge difference.

The goodness and love we leave behind can make an incredible difference in people's lives. Even better is knowing that the goodness and love aren't random occurrences because they "will follow me all the days of my life" (v. 6).

Best of all, it is not up to us in our own strength and sheer willpower to leave a trail of goodness and love. Rather, it is the shepherd's goodness and love first given to us and then given through us that become a legacy of love following us every day.

7

Between Safety and Risk, Always Take the Risk

> I didn't say no because between safety and
> adventure I choose adventure.
>
> Craig Ferguson

There can be no adventure without risk. Now I've said it. It's out in the open, and there is no going back. We might wish and hope it weren't so, but that won't change a thing. Every adventurous step we take can give us purpose, joy, new experiences, and growing faith, but it won't give us a 100 percent guarantee.

"The biggest risk is not taking any risk," Mark Zuckerberg, CEO of Facebook, pointed out. "In a world that is changing really quickly, the only strategy that is guaranteed to fail is not taking risks."[1]

Why do some people take risks to climb mountains or jump out of airplanes (hopefully with a parachute) or swim with sharks? Even though they work and plan and prepare themselves mentally and physically for the challenges ahead, inevitably, they will be faced with the decision to take action. For someone else, the decision to ask their boss for a raise or a promotion is equally risky and also requires preparation, strategy, courage, and the possibility of failure.

People are different when it comes to their ability to tolerate or embrace risk in their lives. The medical community has worked to determine why some people seek risk almost addictively while others prefer to play it safe and maintain the status quo. Research highlights the dopamine levels in our brains and the body's ability to enhance or inhibit the effects of stimulus from risk-oriented actions.

⁕⁕⁕⁕⁕⁕⁕⁕⁕⁕⁕⁕⁕⁕⁕⁕⁕⁕⁕⁕⁕⁕⁕

Every day we have opportunities to choose between safety and risk. The choices we make reveal a lot about our character, values, and the need for control of ourselves and others. Our lives can be shaped by the choices we make, and every choice has a measure of risk to it. Just walking outside has an element of risk to it. Getting in a car or driving a car, or walking down the sidewalk while cars are driven near us, is a calculated risk. So is getting on an airplane, riding a bicycle, or riding a horse. Each has its own measure of risk that we must consider carefully before we choose.

My mother-in-law, Lila, was born in Montreal, then returned to a small village in Ireland, where she spent her childhood. She lived ninety-four years without ever flying on an airplane. That was a risk she wouldn't take. "If my children ever need me, then I'd fly to them," she used to say. But no matter their need, it wasn't enough to get her on a plane. Whenever her children offered a plane ticket so she could come for a visit, her resolute response was, "I'll die before you get me on a plane!" She was right. When she died, the mortuary flew her body to San Diego for burial.

Although Lila chose not to fly, she took other risks of her choice without hesitation. She drove great distances pulling a trailer across the nation's highways, ignoring my warnings of the danger whenever senior citizens pull trailers behind their cars. Perhaps she felt in control with the trailer in tow, while the airplane would most likely be flown by someone she didn't know or trust.

A need for control will lead some people to choose safety rather than risk. The opposite is also true. A need for control motivates some people to take a risk rather than remain in their safe environment. Regardless of which side we choose, safety or risk, the real issue is how much control we really have.

When we sense our control of a situation, our tolerance for risk goes up. Even if we are wrong to think we are controlling the situation, the perception of control can be enough for us to take the risk. This may contribute to the willingness to risk that characterizes most entrepreneurs. The belief that they will be their own boss and control their destiny provides the foundation on which many enterprises are built.

||||||||||||||||||||||||||||||

Of course, not all risks are the same. There are risks we can afford to take. For example, visiting a new restaurant in town is a risk. We might experience bad service, or the food might be poorly prepared, or we might get sick with E. coli, or the people at the table next to us might be annoying. Should we risk it? We may decide to take the risk because if the meal is wonderful, we will enjoy a new experience and have a wonderful night out. This is a risk we may choose because we can afford to.

There are some risks we can't afford to take. The cost of failure would be devastating and could lead to enormous loss. Watching the news one evening, I was shocked to hear of a young couple who mortgaged their home, emptied their savings accounts, and used the money to buy nearly $300,000 of Lotto tickets. So certain of a colossal payoff, they told the reporter it was their "investment" strategy.

Then I remembered a time when my wife and I were a young couple entering graduate school. I foolishly quit my job, took all of our savings, and invested in the commodities market. Eileen was wary and not excited to see me risking all we had on something so nebulous, but the first few weeks were great. I doubled our money in a few transactions. But the third week I lost everything in cocoa futures. I was devastated and embarrassed, and I had only myself to blame. Filled with shame, I don't know how I ever got the courage to tell Eileen the truth about what I had done. Of course, she was horrified that I had lost it all and had jeopardized our entire future because of my foolishness and greed. Some risks we can't afford to take, believe me.

⁞⁞⁞⁞⁞⁞⁞⁞⁞⁞⁞⁞⁞⁞⁞⁞⁞⁞⁞⁞⁞⁞⁞⁞⁞⁞⁞⁞

Though we may tend to see risk taking as something negative or something to be avoided, there are reasons we take action in spite of reservations. Success doesn't happen in a vacuum; we have to pursue it. Not every risk is successful, but many are. "You really have to put one foot in front of the other and start your journey," said Kay Koplovitz, the first female CEO of a television network. "You have to be comfortable that you don't know exactly how you are going to get to the results that you want to see. There is going to be experimentation along the way. And you have to be comfortable that you can think your way through and actually execute your way through to the desired outcome. I expected to be successful. I wanted to be successful."[2] Rather than seeing a risk as a path to failure, we can picture it as an opportunity to succeed.

New opportunities are also discovered when we take risks. When we choose to take a risk, just making the decision helps us overcome our dreaded fear of failure, and we can begin to see that even failure doesn't have to be the end for us. Rather, it can further our growth and lead us forward to new opportunities. We can learn from our mistakes and make wiser choices. We can practice thoughtful decision making that moves us past our comfort zones out into a life of adventure and purpose. Perhaps we are most open to learn and grow when we are in risky situations. Pamela Barnes, president of EngenderHealth, pointed out, "Until we are willing to put ourselves out there and take a risk, we will never be able to achieve professional success and realize our potential. It's time to leave our comfort zone; time to go after what we're passionate about; and time to achieve our dreams."[3]

Creativity increases when we are moving out of our comfort zones and taking calculated risks. Problem-solving skills emerge, and new ideas begin to flow when we are engaged in a new adventure. Old patterns and approaches don't serve us well, but new approaches and fresh ideas feed our creativity. Instead of focusing energy on staying safe, we gain momentum and our confidence grows with each step.

〰〰〰〰〰〰〰〰〰〰〰

Taking a risk is not the same as gambling. We benefit from taking risks when we prepare and educate ourselves about the potential benefits and threats we will encounter. It takes more than wishful thinking and good intentions to thoughtfully plan and carefully implement the necessary steps to reach our goals. Throwing out random ideas and impulsively running from one thing to another may result in occasional success, but it isn't a strategy that will succeed over the long haul.

Management guru Peter Drucker believes that action without thinking is the cause of every failure. Because I'm naturally impulsive, I know I need to take time to prepare and think through what I'm about to do so that I don't take unnecessary risks. Thinking first and acting second helps me minimize the downside of the risks I take. I am also helped by having people in my life who ask good questions that help me think through the best alternatives.

When I was diagnosed with ADHD, I asked the physician what benefit would come from taking Ritalin. He thought for a minute and then said, "It will give you three seconds." I didn't understand his response until he explained. "The medication will give you three seconds between the time you think of something and when you act on it. It may not seem like much time, but when something crosses your mind, you won't just say or do something you might regret. You will have three seconds to choose whether to say or do it." I've learned there is great value in three little seconds.

||||||||||||||||||||||||||||||||||

Perhaps we need to change the way we think about risks. Rather than thinking of them as threats to our security or choices that could bring our world crashing down, we could think of them as important parts of the journey of discovery and growth.

When we look at a risk in context, it may not seem so foreboding. Think about taking a whole year to try something new and different and adventurous. Doing so might seem like a huge risk. But if an average life span is around eighty years, spending a year to see if a bold idea might work is one year out of eighty, or 1.25 percent of a life.[4] Suddenly, the risk seems much smaller. An all-or-nothing mentality prevents people from taking healthy risks, but if we put them in perspective and see them as steps on a journey, we remove the burden and are released to experience an adventure.

Here are some healthy risks that are very much worth taking.

1. Risk getting turned down.

Whenever we ask anyone for anything, we risk getting turned down. Because it hurts to be rejected and we don't want to hurt, we often don't even ask. The request may be big, like asking for a raise or asking someone to marry you, or it could be something small, like asking the person across the table to pass the ketchup. The request may be personal, like asking a person out on a date, or it may be impersonal, like asking for directions when we're lost. If we don't ask, we are the ones who take away any chance of hearing yes.

2. Risk failing.

Don't get me wrong, I hate failing, though I've certainly failed many times. If we don't risk failing, we can never succeed because success demands risking failure. Studies show that while women often regret things they have done, men primarily regret things they didn't do. If we hold back because we don't want to risk failing, we will probably have regrets. This is true whether the regret involves the person we didn't marry, the job we turned down, or the opportunity we passed over because there was no guarantee of success.

3. Risk being misunderstood.

One of the downsides of being creative and pursuing our dreams is that people may question, judge, or mistrust us. Too often we let the fear of being misunderstood block us from pursuing a new idea. It can also inhibit us to the point that we give up on a fresh approach and fall back into old patterns and ways of doing things. What's been working for others may not work for us, and what works for us may not be right for them. The goal is not simply to fit in; it's to discover the best ways of doing things using our own minds and hearts.

Every organization, whether a business or a church, has a built-in defense system that rises up to block creativity and maintain the way things have been. If we risk being misunderstood, we may arrive at a whole new level of growth.

4. Risk saying, "I love you."

As I was talking with a tall, serious-looking man after church, he looked intently at me and said, "Pastor, I love my wife so much, I almost told her." Though he didn't crack a smile, I imagine he was laughing hysterically inside at this old joke.

It is risky to put our feelings out in the open when the other person may not respond the way we hoped. Just imagine if we say, "I love you," and they don't say it back. No one wants to experience that terrible feeling. But it is pretty exciting when we hear those words in return. Maybe the other person is hoping we will make the first move. Even if they don't feel the same way, at least our feelings are out in the open and we can move on without false hopes or wondering what might have been.

5. Risk being yourself.

Who we are, what we have experienced, and what we believe make us unique and unlike anyone else in the entire world. When we share ourselves honestly, it is a gift of great value. We are often tempted to hide behind masks to appear the way we think others want us to be. But hiding not only cheats them but also cheats us out of a chance to show our true colors. In relationships, being ourselves may be difficult, but it is necessary. If someone knows the real us, they can love the real us. Unless we take this risk, we may never know we are loved as we are.

6. Risk not being good enough.

Regardless of what we attempt, there is a chance we won't be good enough. Is that so bad? Sometimes it can be freeing to learn we just aren't good enough. That doesn't mean we are a bad person, or worthless, or even good for nothing. It just means we aren't good enough in this situation, with these people, at this time. Sure, we'll feel crummy for a while, but in everything we do, we'll either be good enough or not good enough, and it's all right to know which.

In my early years, I had a dream of being like my country western singing and songwriting hero Kris Kristofferson. I wanted to play guitar, travel in a band, and have a great life. I assumed I could do it, because he made it all seem so effortless. I worked hard, played in some bands, owned a guitar store, and taught guitar for several years. I even played on a couple of albums. I assumed music would be my life. Except for one tiny detail: I wasn't good enough. No matter my sincerity or how hard I worked at being a musician, there was always someone else who played a lot better. I recognized the reality of my limited ability in music and went a different direction. The irony is that in some ways my life did turn out the way I dreamed it would. I still got to travel the country and be in front of crowds, not singing but speaking, and not encouraging people through songs I had written but through books I had written. If I hadn't found out I wasn't good enough at one thing, I might never have realized I was good enough at something else.

7. Risk being good enough.

Where did we get the idea that we must be expert, competent, capable, and perfect in all things? The need to be perfect can destroy our lives. Perfectionism stops us from taking even the first step forward. It stifles our creativity and keeps our dreams from coming true. It may be only a little voice in our head, but it has the power to heap scorn and rebuke on our efforts.

"Perfectionism tells us that to move ahead, we must first be perfect," writes Julia Cameron. "And yet, it is often perfectionism that stalls us and keeps us from moving ahead at all. Perfectionism is the opposite of humility, which allows us to move slowly and steadily forward, making and learning from our mistakes. Perfectionism says do it 'right'—or not at all."[5]

Whenever I get bogged down in a project trying to get everything just so, I try to remember the wisdom of G. K. Chesterton: "Anything worth doing is worth doing badly."[6] He understood that good enough is good enough. Besides, nothing is intended to be perfect this side of heaven.

8. Risk getting hurt.

In small, seemingly insignificant ways and in large, impactful ways, getting hurt is an unavoidable part of living. It hurts when the person we trusted lets us down. Our hearts will be broken, and unfortunately, we will break someone else's heart. We might be tempted to protect ourselves by saying, "I don't care." But if we try to protect ourselves in order to avoid getting hurt, we might end up missing out on happiness as well. Marc Chernoff writes, "Anybody who is capable of living and loving is bound to get hurt at some point, but that's a risk that's well worth the reward. The result is a life filled with honesty and love. So take too many pictures, laugh too much, and love like you've never been hurt. Don't be afraid that your days will end in pain, be afraid they will never begin with honesty and love."[7]

It can be hard to take a risk when we are sorting through the life debris from everything going wrong. I remember thinking how I'd never let myself get in another situation in which I wasn't in control or people could let me down. I didn't want to risk getting involved in people's lives because it hurt too much if I was rejected. Fortunately, some friends helped me overcome my reservations and my desire to maintain control. I'm grateful for their courage when I had very little, for their vision when mine was disabled, and for their unwavering commitment to me and the adventure that was waiting for me just ahead. They took a chance on me so that in time I could once more take a chance on me.

||||||||||||||||||||||||||||||||

The opposite of faith is not doubt—it is control. Faith requires stepping out of our comfort zones and letting God lead us forward into an uncertain future. Abraham was invited to leave his father's house and take his family on a journey. Imagine how he might have felt when he asked God where they were going. "To the land I will show you" (Gen. 12:1) was an answer that may not have filled Abraham with confidence. I doubt he had an easy time trying to explain it to his wife, Sarah, either.

When Jesus called his first disciples to leave their family business in the fishing industry and follow him, I wonder if their father, Zebedee, like Ricky Ricardo, responded, "You got some splainin' to do." As far as we can tell, Jesus didn't sit down and explain the plan for their travels, nor did he give hints about some of the basics, like where are we going? Who will we see? What will we eat? Where will we stay? Perhaps this was because faith isn't needed when everything is spelled out for us.

Will every risk be successful? Of course not. But God calls us, like Abraham, like the disciples, to step out in faith, knowing he is with us. And we can be assured that the risks he asks us to take will bring adventure and with it the possibility of a better tomorrow that is very different from today.

8

Giving People the Weapons That Can Hurt Us

Nothing makes us so lonely as our secrets.

Paul Tournier

I have yet to meet someone who didn't claim to value authenticity. Advertising reminds us "It's the real thing," passing remarks challenge us to "get real," and books describing what the next generation is seeking mention authenticity as one of its highest values. At first glance, it seems authenticity is something everyone embraces. Except it isn't.

Realistically, our culture, our cities, and the places we work, shop, and play put very little value on authenticity. The idea of being real is great. We find it easy to talk about the importance of being real, vulnerable, and honest. So how come the authenticity we hold up as an important value is so rarely experienced on a daily basis? Perhaps we value the idea of being real but not the reality of it.

Imagine working for a company that has affirmed its commitment to honest communication and authentic relationships in the workplace. Now, sitting in your performance review at work, you say to your supervisor, "I'd like to be real with you, so I need to tell you that I feel as if I'm way over my head at work. To be honest, sometimes I don't think I even know what I'm doing here, so I try to pick up clues from the people around me and hope I don't mess up too badly. I'm saying this to you because I know how much our company values honest communication."

How would that kind of authenticity be received? Probably not very well, I imagine.

A failure to be authentic is not just a problem in the workplace; it is also a dilemma in the church. On the surface, it seems that churches would value and encourage honest, vulnerable sharing, but that is unfortunately not the reality of most people's experience. I learned this at an early stage of my development.

Our family would drive thirty miles from our home in Whittier to Los Angeles for church, and the entire way my dad would be swatting us over the back of the car seat, telling us to be quiet and keep our hands to ourselves, while the four of us kids would argue, poke, fight, and tease each other. As my dad parked the car, he'd warn us to wipe off those tears, put a smile on our faces, and keep what had happened in the car in the car. So we'd run off to Sunday school, where we'd meet with other kids who were pretending everything was great and dishonesty was the rule of the day.

This kind of pretense continues in adulthood, so now we go into church hoping no one will find out who we really are and what we are really going through in our lives.

I believe in vulnerability even when I'm not completely at ease with it and whether or not I'm willing to be vulnerable. In fact, as a pastor, I want all the members of our church to share authentically. Hopefully, they'll share among themselves, but if not, they are welcome to share with me. Sadly, the sharing has not always been mutual. Ministers have listened to confessions of church members for hundreds of years, but we tend not to reciprocate by authentically sharing with them our struggles and sins.

One author who addresses this issue is John Powell in his marvelous book *Why Am I Afraid to Tell You Who I Am?*[1] It isn't a long, complicated book. In fact, it has large type, wide margins, and drawings about every other page, but that doesn't lessen the importance of his message. He concludes that the reason we are afraid of honesty and openness in our relationships is because if I tell you who I am and you don't like me, that will hurt. So we cover up and hide our real selves as protection against hurt and rejection. After all, if I pretend to be a certain way and you don't like me, I can always comfort myself with the assurance that you don't really know me.

Reading Powell's book as a young adult was eye-opening for me. Like most of the people I knew, I had become adept at pretending to be the person I thought others wanted me to be. I must have been a pretty good actor because I fooled a lot of people. All the while, the fear of being known was growing in me.

When we are afraid of being known, we don't want people to get too close because they might see us warts and all and not like us. We all have sensitive areas in our lives that we don't want others to know about. Many of us have secrets that might harm us if they become known. Giving people the weapons that can hurt us goes against our deep-seated tendencies for self-protection.

llllllllllllllllllllllllllllll

To protect ourselves, we conceal our failures, weaknesses, and frustrations, hoping that if they remain buried for long enough, they might simply go away. But they don't go away. Rather than diminishing to the point of disappearing, our secrets grow stronger, until they begin to consume us. The opposite is also true. The things we confess or share openly lose their power over us. When we share a problem, a personal struggle, or even a failure from the past, it loses its grip on us and its power over us is lessened. Maybe this could explain why the Bible invites us to "confess your sins to each other" (James 5:16).

We are flooded with well-meaning advice to conceal our weaknesses and flaws and to accentuate our strengths. An emphasis on self-esteem, positive imaging, and whatever the latest motivational speakers are selling culminates in people who posture and pose for one another, striving to present a good image of themselves, all the while being consumed by obsessive-compulsive behavior as they try to keep a lid on the secrets festering just below the surface of their lives. Our secrets control us and our strengths lose their effectiveness simply because we have adopted a strategy that is a complete reversal of what Jesus taught his disciples.

Of course, there are many ways to avoid authenticity and to keep from giving people the weapons that can hurt us. Besides hiding our flaws, there is the strategy of trying to figure out what kind of person others want us to be and then trying to become that person. The problem with this coping mechanism is that some people want us to be one way while others want us to be a different way. Pretty soon we are acting different ways depending on who we are with. Like Mrs. Doubtfire frantically changing clothes and personas in the restaurant bathroom, we find it difficult to remember who we are supposed to be, with which people, at which times.

When I was with people who wanted me to be vulnerable, I became good at faux sharing. I could appear to be vulnerable and authentic, but I really wasn't. I became adept at sharing personal stories to make it seem as if I was opening myself up, but they were usually from my past and not about what I was dealing with in the present. When I shared those old stories, people appreciated my openness without realizing I was diverting attention away from the struggles and issues I was currently having. Though my stories were true and my sharing was personal, very few people realized I was not allowing them to know the real me.

We've become accustomed to hearing about people who struggled mightily in their lives but found success, love, and peace. Sometimes I think about what a wonderful story I could tell if my life had been different. I might have been a famous motivational speaker if only I could say, "I was once a terrible person. I used drugs and went out and killed people. But in prison I met Jesus, and now my life is great—all my problems are solved and I'm trouble-free!" Wow, I could travel the country giving speeches, maybe write a bestseller, and get interviewed by Oprah!

While it's true we all have a past that can be important to share with others, it's also true we all have a now that must also be shared.

‖‖‖‖‖‖‖‖‖‖‖‖‖‖‖‖‖‖‖‖‖‖‖

Paul, writing in 2 Corinthians, reminds us that we are all like damaged pottery. We all have cracks that make us less valuable and less useful. He goes on to point out that our value is not in ourselves but in the reality of Jesus's presence in us, which gives us meaning and value regardless of our condition.

In 2 Corinthians 6, he writes, "We put no stumbling block in anyone's path, so that our ministry will not be discredited. Rather, as servants of God we commend ourselves in every way: in great endurance; in troubles, hardships and distresses; in beatings, imprisonments and riots; in hard work, sleepless nights and hunger" (vv. 3–5). This passage makes me wonder, "That is how they commend themselves? Who wants to hear about that? Their experiences certainly don't sound very positive."

I have a friend who for many years was the pastor of a well-known megachurch. Whenever we got together for lunch, he always started the conversation the same way. "How's it going, John? Tell me only the good stuff!" Now, for an enthusiastically negative person like me, that left me with very little to share. One time I finally just opened up and shared about a current struggle I was having and how painful it seemed to me. He listened quietly until I stopped to take a bite of salad. Then he softly asked, "That is the good stuff?"

I laughed and then told him that in the midst of this painful time I was still trusting God and hoping for good to come out of the pain. He thought about my response for a second, and then a smile came over his face. "You're right, that is very good." I guess our view all depends on our definition of "only the good stuff."

The apostle Paul commends himself by sharing about trouble, hardship, imprisonments, beatings, and riots, which are all things I would probably want to hide if I was trying to make a good impression. Yet he brings them up, perhaps because he wants his readers to know him for who he really is.

How can we begin to share authentically and vulnerably without overwhelming the people around us? We certainly don't want to be guilty of premature disclosure or inappropriate sharing.

Paul shows us a way to relate authentically without being inappropriate. Right after mentioning the riots, beatings, and sleepless nights, he reminds us that he is going through these things "in purity, understanding, patience and kindness; in the Holy Spirit and in sincere love; in truthful speech and in the power of God" (2 Cor. 6:6–7).

We don't have to hide our real selves. We can be honest about our lives and share truthfully. We can start to demonstrate that it is possible to trust God in the real stuff we are going through. In the midst of real pain and struggles, we can share openly, truthfully, with love and kindness through the power of God.

I live in Seattle, which by most standards is a pretty unique town. In my travels, I meet many people who all say the same thing: "I hear Seattle is pretty and it rains a lot, but I've never been there." This sums up the knowledge and experience most people have regarding the Pacific Northwest. And to some extent they are correct. It is beautiful when it's not raining, but it rains all the time.

Something that many people don't know about Seattle is that it is also a city with one of the lowest church attendance statistics in the country. There is a subtle rejection of anything that might be construed as Christian. Most of the people I know have never been to church, and many of those don't know many people who have ever gone to church. Sometimes they try to relate to me by telling me they once had an aunt who was religious. Of course, she was the eccentric one in the family. At wedding receptions, I often get seated next to her for some unexplained reason.

Our pagan culture doesn't surprise me because I assume most people have very little experience or few relationships with authentic Christians. Perhaps their indifference toward or rejection of Christianity is influenced by experiences with phony Christians they have met. Imagine what might happen if we began to share personally and authentically with the people around us?

We could honestly talk about what is going on in our lives and that we don't know how we'll get through it without God's help. Authentic sharing without simple answers can be startling in its realness. Telling someone we don't know how things will turn out and yet we're going to see what the Lord might do in our circumstance opens the door for honest sharing.

I've observed that many of the programs designed to teach people how to share their faith, which are widely used in churches, are based on training participants to give quick and confident answers. They rarely seem grounded in authentic sharing. The one thing we might do that could be transformational in people's lives is often the one thing we don't do.

The apostle Paul shared vulnerably. "I was beaten but I wasn't killed, I was sorrowful but still rejoicing, I was poor but others were getting rich, I had nothing but I had everything." He goes through his entire list and then says, "We have spoken freely to you . . . and opened wide our hearts to you. We are not withholding our affection from you, but you are withholding yours from us" (2 Cor. 6:11–12). I totally get that. Have you ever been vulnerable with someone, sharing openly and honestly, only to have them respond stiffly with a nice, appropriate, safe answer?

Recently, Eileen and I went on a cruise to the Caribbean to celebrate our anniversary. Cruises can be strange experiences because on a cruise everyone's life is perfect. The second day out we met a couple who exuded "cruise ship happiness," which may have been magnified by the abundance of adult beverages they were drinking.

At one point, the husband leaned over as if to share a great secret with me and loudly proclaimed, "We've been married forty-five years, and we've never had a disagreement or argument!" Beaming, he asked his wife, who was sitting quietly at the table, to show us pictures of their children, all of whom I learned were brilliant, talented, successful, and good-looking. I pictured them driving around with bumper stickers on the backs of their cars reminding everyone that "Our child is an honor student at Podunk Elementary School." I started to feel sorry for them, since they obviously didn't really know each other. Forty-five years together without honestly sharing with each other, bobbing along on the surface of a relationship, avoiding intimacy. Sadly, I thought, they probably didn't even know their kids on a deep level. It crossed my mind that their home might be the loneliest house on the block.

Although they never asked about us, we also were celebrating our forty-fifth anniversary, except our experience was nothing like theirs, and I can't remember a day we didn't have a disagreement or two. Our relationship was a struggle from the beginning. We spent the first twenty-three years in marriage counseling and seemed on the edge of not making it for at least sixteen of those years. Staying together forty-five years was a miracle worth celebrating.

Walking back to our cabin that evening, we were grateful we didn't have to pretend life was perfect or even trouble-free. Our life was not easy, but it was authentic, and it was good.

||||||||||||||||||||||||||||||

My friend Bill once asked me if I had any personal relationships with people outside the churches I pastored. I made up an excuse about not having enough time since I was so busy trying to meet the needs of my parishioners. He told me about his boat racing adventures and how this hobby had opened the door to a new circle of mostly secular friends. "You need something like that in your life that will keep you involved with real people outside the church." When I told him I enjoyed playing golf, though I'm not very good, he suggested I join a golf club in my community. I told him I might be insecure around so many people who appear successful and trouble-free. "That's how most people feel about coming into our churches," he said. "They think we have it together and they might not fit in." Then he said, "Try it as an experiment, and just be yourself."

I kept thinking about Bill's challenge, not knowing if I had the courage to move beyond my comfort zone in the church, but I wanted to give it a try. Finally, I decided to join a golf club. I picked an old, classic country club that had been formed in 1911, with a rich history and heritage in the community.

My first obstacle was getting into the club. I knew only one social member, so I invited her to lunch and asked if she would sponsor me in the membership process. She was happy to do so but soon discovered that social members couldn't sponsor golf memberships. Further, two respected golfing members had to sign an affidavit stating that they had personally known a candidate for at least five years and that the candidate was someone they knew, respected, and trusted to be the kind of person who would meet the highest standards expected of club members.

Realizing there was no way I'd be able to qualify for membership, I started to thank my friend for her efforts. She stopped me and said she would look into the situation. In a couple days, I heard she had turned in my application showing that I was being sponsored by two of the most respected members of the club. All I had to do was wait the allotted time to see if any members objected to my membership and be approved by the vetting committee. It was while sitting in the meeting with the vetting committee that I met my sponsors for the first time.

Now I'm not saying the club is a little stiff and uppity, but on my first day as a new member, the club pro stopped me and informed me that I would have to wear a different shirt because of the dress code. Having read the rule about needing to wear a shirt with a collar, I pointed out that mine had a collar. "But it's a Hawaiian shirt," he said with disdain.

"Yes, it is," I told him with a smile, "and in Hawaii it's just called a shirt!"

The first thing I noticed was that everyone I met looked good and appeared quite successful in every area of their lives. I was tempted to pretend that I was too (except for the looking good part) in order to blend in and be accepted. But since I'd promised Bill I would be myself and not pretend to be something I wasn't, I fought the temptation to fake it.

Of course, I made an effort to be kind and genuinely interested in people as we got to know each other. Then things began to happen. After sharing with someone about our son's struggle with addiction, I received a call from the man's wife. She was encouraging and honest as she connected in a caring way with our family. She kindly offered some resources they had found helpful in dealing with similar issues and encouraged us one parent to another. Since then, when playing golf with the husband, sometimes our conversations turn to personal sharing as we walk along. The other day my new friend called out from across the golf course letting me know that he and his wife had ordered one of my books, which they would be reading together.

In time, more and more people began to open up about their lives and struggles. One couple shared the pain of losing a child, another person was struggling with his faith, another was going through a painful time in his marriage. There were stories about children with challenges, broken dreams, and business crises that were discussed in the parking lot, in the locker room, and in far corners of the dining room.

One afternoon as I was walking to my car, a young man approached. He said he had heard a rumor that I had written a book about getting past what we'll never get over, and I told him I was impressed he was able to remember such a complicated title. He was young, handsome, successful, and a scratch golfer to boot. At that moment, I was a little jealous of him and wished my life could be as easy and trouble-free as his seemed to be. Suddenly, he looked around and quietly said, "Three months ago my life came to a crashing halt, and I don't know how to go on from here. Maybe we could get together and talk."

I'm learning that others will be authentic and vulnerable to the extent that we are authentic and vulnerable. Thus, our candid sharing can open the door for others to share as well. We must keep in mind that not everyone can handle the truth and not every response will be positive, but that doesn't matter because we will be healthier for sharing.

Bill was right. There's no need to pretend or posture to impress people. Simply honestly sharing our lives with someone else is a powerful gift. It is a gift that can impact our relationships in profound ways.

Vulnerability is giving other people the weapons that can hurt us. We choose to give because we care, and we hope they won't turn and use the things we've shared against us. We know that some people will betray us, and it might hurt a lot. But we keep on being real because it is the only way to be free and healthy.

9

Eat More Ice Cream
and Fewer Beans

I know not all that may be coming, but be it
what it will, I'll go to it laughing.

Herman Melville

Accountability is one of the most misused words in the English language. I spent years believing I needed more accountability in my life. Being me, I assumed, was a big problem that needed fixing. Of course, all through the years there were plenty of scolding voices around to remind me that I could really benefit from some firm accountability. But the idea of checking in with someone like a moral gym coach with a clipboard and a whistle didn't fill me with joy.

Who hijacked accountability and turned it into such a negative, demoralizing weapon of mass distraction? Maybe it's time for an accountability revolution. When everything goes wrong, we don't need anyone pointing out our failures and shortcomings. We are already aware of them, trust me. What we may have trouble seeing is anything good, worthy, or valuable about our lives. Wouldn't it be great to have accountability for those things?

While meeting with someone I respected and wanted to impress, I told him about some of the things I was working on, the difficulty I was having when it came to solving problems, and how much time and energy went into these heroic efforts. He listened without interrupting, and when I got to the end, I asked for his input.

"I think you should eat more ice cream and fewer beans," he said with a smile. Then probably noticing my confused expression, he went on, "You didn't even mention having fun or relaxing. If you've completely stopped playing and just slog through work, you're going to miss out on a lot of life."

As we talked about this, he suggested I find people who would hold me accountable for more fun in life. Though the idea seemed weird at first, the more I thought about it, the more it made sense. Maybe I needed accountability after all. But instead of keeping track of my mistakes, these people would encourage me not to take myself so seriously and to lighten up instead. I'd never thought of accountability for those things. Maybe I did need encouragement to be more fun to be around. After all, even I wouldn't want to hang out with me when I'm tired, stressed, and feeling sorry for myself. Why would anyone else want to be with *that* me?

In the Gospels, it is apparent that most of the criticism Jesus received involved his willingness to eat a lot more ice cream than beans. The religious leaders, his family, and even cousin John (the Baptist) were confused and dismayed that

Jesus and his followers were having too much fun, hanging out with the wrong people, and not staying focused on the right things. I guess from their perspective, way too much ice cream was being consumed.

Our tendency to criticize rather than affirm can be such a part of our relating that we don't even notice that it is happening. I am sometimes surprised to realize the silliness of my negativity. For example, I'm a terrible gardener. I admit it, and everyone who hangs around me knows it. Of course, people who are good at growing and cultivating things have tried to fix me by giving me tips and words of encouragement, but even they eventually gave up, assuming I was a lost cause. But I keep trying.

Last year I bought three tomato plants that looked prosperous and hopeful. I put two in the ground and one in a hanging upside-down contraption that I found at Home Depot. Can you guess how plentiful the harvest was after all my good intentions and well-meaning efforts? Exactly three! Not three bushels or even three pounds. Just three tomatoes.

I started thinking how lazy and uncooperative these plants were, perhaps even selfish, though we shouldn't assume motives. My first idea was to go out and scold the plants for their bad behavior. Maybe a stern talking-to and a lecture on how they should try harder would be beneficial. If they worked harder, showed more conviction, and demonstrated a more positive attitude, they certainly would be more fruitful.

But then I decided that probably wasn't the most effective strategy because scolding and lecturing plants, like people, rarely makes them more fruitful. Perhaps if I had watered or fertilized them, or moved them into the sunshine, it would have made a difference.

While it seems ridiculous to scold plants to make them produce, isn't it amazing how often we do it to ourselves and sometimes even to those we love when we are hurting or lacking something in our lives?

||||||||||||||||||||||||||||||||

Where did we get the idea that if we enjoy something or love what we are doing, it must not be right? There are times we are like the stern villagers in the film *Babette's Feast* who were invited to a gourmet banquet prepared as a gift of love by the young chef who had moved to their island. Walking into the beautiful, festive room, they warn each other not to let on if they find themselves accidently enjoying the feast.

This negative view can seep into our thinking in subtle ways. For much of my life, I assumed that God's will for me was something difficult, unpleasant, and destined to make me miserable. I harbored the quiet fear that if I let Jesus into my life, he would send me somewhere scary and strange like Africa as a missionary. Of course, since I had lived in Africa as a child with parents who had actually gone there as missionaries, it wasn't a totally unreasonable fear, but you see my point.

I decided to find out what people really think about God's will, so I made up a phony survey. During a two-week period, I surveyed people by asking only one question. "If you were given a choice between something you would love to do and something that would be hard and unpleasant for you, which one do you think God would want you to choose?"

Would you be shocked to learn most people picked the hard one? I guess there is an assumption that God wants us to be miserable. No wonder we hesitate when it comes to putting our faith in God. If we believe he wants us to be miserable, why should we trust him? This misunderstanding is widely held even though it is very wrong!

"Every day God invites us on the same kind of adventure," writes Bob Goff. "It's not a trip where He sends us a rigid itinerary. He simply invites us. God asks us what it is He's made us to love, what it is that captures our attention, what feeds that deep indescribable need of our souls to experience the richness of the world He made. And then, leaning over us, He whispers, 'Let's go do that together.'"[1]

||||||||||||||||||||||||||||||

The truth is, God doesn't want us to be miserable. He made us, loves us, knows us, and wants us to experience his mercy and tenderness. When the Bible teaches us to "love your neighbor as yourself" (Matt. 22:39), it is an invitation to show mercy to those around us in the same way we are merciful to ourselves. The problem is how little mercy we have for ourselves. Our biggest joy killer is not out there somewhere; it is right inside us. If only we would open the floodgates of mercy and treat ourselves and others with tenderness rather than harsh criticism, our experience of joy would know no bounds.

The Beatitudes help us see how we can live freely and passionately and not be bound up and limited by our attitudes and behaviors toward ourselves and others.

In the Sermon on the Mount, Jesus taught, "Blessed are the merciful, for they will be shown mercy" (Matt. 5:7). This is the only beatitude in which the reward, or the payoff, is the same as the action we are asked to do. Because of God's great care for us and his love and tender mercy, we are able to turn to people around us and treat them with mercy. We can show others some of the kindness and tenderness that God is showing to us. When we put this idea into action and demonstrate merciful compassion to others, Jesus says, the reward we receive is more mercy for ourselves. Life becomes a giant circle in which mercy flows without end as we receive it, give it away, and receive more.

Mercy is one of the great words in the Bible. Throughout Scripture, the word *mercy* is used to describe God's tender compassion for us, including the way he relates to us in love and grace.

Jesus said we are to treat people with this same tender mercy, compassion, and love. This must have been important to Jesus because many of his teaching parables were about mercy. There was the man who was forgiven a great debt. Then walking home relieved and joyful, he sees a friend who owes him a small, insignificant amount. He grabs his friend and begins to choke him and beat him while demanding that he be paid in full.

Jesus taught that if we've been given a great gift of mercy, we are in the same manner to give it to people around us. It is to be our first course of action, not an afterthought.

My uncle Fred was a survivor of the death camps during the Holocaust. During World War II, Germany's Nazis openly hated the Jews, and because they hated them, they were cruel to them. They were mean and violent and abusive in their treatment of these neighbors. The more they were cruel to the Jews, the more they hated them.

This happens not just in history but also in our contemporary communities. When we identify groups of people to hate or blame for our lack of good fortune, we soon treat them disdainfully and cruelly. When we treat them this way, we hate them even more. This same phenomenon can happen inside of us in very personal ways. Something happens and we begin to hate an aspect of ourselves, and soon we act in hateful and hurtful ways toward ourselves. We begin to do self-destructive things to ourselves, and we demean, criticize, and sabotage ourselves. We find ourselves undermining the very things we want to experience, and with every mistreatment of ourselves, we hate ourselves even more. Then instead of the biblical picture of receiving mercy, giving mercy, and receiving more mercy, we have a different experience. Our circle is hatred, undermining, hatred, abuse without end. What we receive from God we need to give to others and to ourselves. Those who are merciful will receive mercy. This is the circle that can obliterate the piercing pain of self-destruction.

Whenever I spend time with people who have self-destructive behaviors, a part of me is tempted to simply tell them to cut it out. But inevitably, as we delve below the surface, it becomes apparent that something happened in them or to them that led them to believe they weren't lovable or worthy of love. Then one thing led to another, and now they find themselves hopeless and bogged down in pain, sadness, anxiety, and shame, which can lead them to hate who they are. Self-hate is like an undertow that pulls them toward more pain, and so the decline goes on and on until they are unable to recognize the cause and effect at work within their own hearts and minds.

<hr/>

God's attitude toward us is loving-kindness, compassionate mercy. Romans 12 begins by saying, "In view of God's mercy... offer your bodies as a living sacrifice" (v. 1). Mercy is God's essential attitude toward us. Because of his mercy, our response is to show up. That is worship. We are present in his presence.

Then Romans 12:2 says, "Do not conform to the pattern of this world, but be transformed by the renewing of your mind." When we are bogged down and the critical voices in our heads are pounding us with judgmental accusations, it's easy to be haunted by our mistakes. This is the world pushing us into its mold. We need a radical interruption. We need a renewal of the mind. We need to stop listening to the self-defeating messages we tell ourselves, and we need to renew our minds with the message and reality of self-compassion. Self-compassion silences the inner critical voice and releases us to be compassionate to others, and it frees us to come out of isolation and engage openly and meaningfully in community. We no longer have to be locked into certain ways of thinking or acting.

We've had many influences in our lives. These influences can motivate us, but they can also hold us back if our thoughts are locked in and maintained by unhealthiness. If that is the case, we need a new way of thinking. This is a biblical concept, but it is also sound from a psychological perspective. Psychiatrist Albert Ellis developed a mode of therapy that became known as rational-emotive therapy. It is grounded in the premise that if we want to change a person's life, we must change the way they think. If they change the way they think, they will discover new ways to respond to emotional stimuli, and relationships, communication, and perceptions will be transformed. But this all begins with a renewal of the mind.

|||||||||||||||||||||||||||||||

Why do we so often struggle to experience God's mercy in our lives? Perhaps it's because so many of us have an assumption that God is mad at us. We are afraid to let God get too close.

Through the years I've had countless conversations with people whose issues eventually led me to tell them that God is not like their earthly parent. If their dad was angry, aloof, critical, absent, or indifferent, it wasn't a difficult leap for them to unconsciously assume that their heavenly Father is the same. But God is not like their dad. The big difference is that God wants to demonstrate tenderness and mercy and compassion in every aspect of our lives. If we will let him. Then our minds can be transformed, and, thinking in a new way, we no longer need to please people or try desperately to gain their approval. Kris Kristofferson was right when he said, "If you try to please other people, you will pay a terrible price in your soul."[2]

The old thinking clouds our minds and brings confusion. We have cloudy, confused thinking about ourselves that pulls us down in shame and discouragement. The old thinking clouds our thinking about others, pulling us into prejudice and stereotyping and hating those who are different from us.

Romans 12 goes on to tell us, "Do not think of yourself more highly than you ought, but rather think of yourself with sober judgment, in accordance with the faith God has distributed to each of you" (v. 3). This is a call to reassess our self-esteem in light of the mercy we have received. Self-esteem alone can never be the true measure of our health because it can easily be distorted. Perhaps this is why narcissists often have extremely high self-esteem, even as they have a condition that twists and distorts their perceptions of themselves and others.

||||||||||||||||||||||||||||

Over the years, I've been involved with many kinds of people. Some were kind and sincere; others were abrupt or demanding. There were those who were easy to be with, and we laughed and enjoyed our times together.

Of course there were always some people who were difficult to be with. I call these folks "joy killers" who use structure, rules, tradition, and fear to bully others into quiet submission. Because conformity is one of their key goals, any efforts to be creative, fun, or empowering are looked on with disdain.

I don't think they are bad people per se. It is just that their hardened attitudes, rigid fixations, and desperate need to be right can turn them into rules police who find a way to suck the air out of a room just by walking in the door.

I've had the displeasure of working with people who are joy killers, and I found it difficult, if not impossible, to maintain a relaxed, joyful, and creative spirit. When we find ourselves relating to people like this, it doesn't take long before we begin feeling guilty, inadequate, or even incompetent. A spirit of distrust surrounds us so that even when we do something that might seem helpful or positive, it is construed as negative or inappropriate.

Maybe this was happening in an incident involving a cafeteria worker at an Idaho public school who was terminated after giving a student a $1.70 lunch. According to the *Idaho Statesman*, Dalene Bowden was put on unpaid leave after giving a twelve-year-old student who said she did not have money a free lunch.

"This just breaks my heart," she told the newspaper. "I was in the wrong, but what do you do when the kid tells you that they're hungry and they don't have any money? I handed her the tray." She also offered to pay for the $1.70 lunch, but her supervisor placed her on leave until the matter could be discussed by the Pocatello/Chubbuck School District.

When the school district sent a letter informing Dalene that she was fired, a Facebook group, "Give Dalene Bowden her job back," formed to support her. They posted a photo of the letter, which stated, "The reason for your termination is due to your theft—stealing school district or another's property and inaccurate transactions when ordering, receiving and serving food." It shouldn't have been a surprise when the school district was deluged with thousands of letters, emails, and phone calls protesting the treatment of the lunch lady. Reluctantly, they reconsidered their action and said she could return to work, "just because it's Christmas."[3]

Before we start looking at everyone around us and trying to identify the relational anarchists or the joy killers in our lives, we need to understand how many times we take on those unhealthy qualities when dealing with ourselves. We don't need others to treat us that way because we find ways to undermine our creativity, derail our plans, and shut down our joy all by ourselves.

I always smile when I see that sign in gift shop windows that says, "Beatings will continue until morale improves." It reminds me how frequently we use a wrongheaded approach on ourselves. I don't think anyone in the history of civilization has been able to force joy onto another person or onto themselves. Yet how often, when we aren't experiencing joy, do we bear down, work harder, and practice being more disciplined, assuming our efforts will make us more joyful. Then when we don't find the result we want, we feel guilty for not doing better or trying hard enough. We don't need others to make us feel guilty; we are doing a fine job ourselves.

Self-improvement can be a slippery slope. We all want to improve and become better versions of ourselves. We also would like to avoid the disapproval of people who want us to change. Usually we start out innocently enough, setting a goal or wanting to do something to better our lives. No one ever tells us that self-improvement can become a virtual slip 'n slide into a pit of dissatisfaction and negativity, with one thing always leading to another and no end in sight.

The other day I was thinking about ways to improve myself, and the first thing that came to mind was changing my diet. I don't mean going on a diet; I've tried many different ones and they never seem to work for me. Once I went on the Atkins diet because I could eat lots of meat, which seemed doable to me. Everything was going fine until the night I ate two whole chickens and realized this diet wasn't going to help me.

So I didn't want to diet but I did want to eat healthier and smarter. I saw a book at Barnes and Noble that was filled with recipes for green shakes. These consisted of various grass clippings mixed with weeds and things like kale and spinach. I bought a special type of blender that was shaped like a giant bullet, and I started whirling and blending my way toward happiness. I even bought a carton of protein shakes at Costco. They tasted a little like chocolate-flavored chemical waste, but I was confident they were better for me than regular food.

In the midst of my green shake experiment, I took a selfie at the local golf course and posted it on Facebook. Most of the comments surprised me. "You certainly look scruffy." "Your beard seems rangy. Time to trim it?" "Hey, tuck your shirt in!" Most of these comments were from my friends, so I thought I'd better take what they said seriously and do something about them.

Right away I considered buying a small grooming comb that has tiny teeth. I could wet my beard and use the comb every day until my beard was trained not to look scruffy anymore. It might take a long time, but I hoped it would be worth the effort. Then I thought perhaps I could improve my appearance by spending more time polishing my shoes before I went out to face the day.

But wait, if I really wanted to make a difference, I needed to figure out my socks. Going to my closet, I found not just one sock drawer but three, plus a bag of loose ones. No wonder nothing ever matched. But I wanted to improve, so if I was going to go to the trouble of having nicely shined shoes, I needed matching socks to go with them.

Later that day, while having lunch with my friend Dave, I broke a tooth. He suggested going to the dentist where his wife, Diane, is the hygienist. After I explained to the receptionist about my broken tooth emergency, I got in right away. Very quickly I could see that Diane was distressed at the condition of my teeth. Evidently, I was not caring for them properly. She advised me to buy a Sonicare device. It's like a fancy electric toothbrush that she assured me would make a big difference. So I went back to Costco and got one. I thought it might vibrate my head off, but I wanted to be a better man, so I committed to giving it a try.

Then I read an article online that said we need to exercise if we don't want our brains to deteriorate. I certainly didn't want my brain to deteriorate. They recommended walking five miles a day to stay sharp mentally. So I considered walking five miles every day, maybe before I used the Sonicare device.

But I really needed to spend some quality time every day journaling. As a discipline, I could get up early and journal for an hour before walking five miles and Sonicaring my teeth. Then I'd put on my perfectly matched socks and shiny shoes, all the while thinking about the green shake waiting for me at the end of the day.

But then I thought about how I wasn't very good at computers. I wanted to blog more and be more proficient with technology, and I definitely needed to update my website. I could enroll in classes at our local college on how to use computers and get really good at blogging. But what I was really interested in was taking some cooking classes. They would be more fun. Besides, I could learn healthier ways to cook. Maybe cooking classes could help me improve my cooking so I wouldn't need the green shakes anymore.

What I really missed was reading. I used to read a lot, but lately I hadn't been reading as much. I thought I should get a couple of good books and keep them handy so I could read when I came back from my daily walk. Yet I felt my life would be enriched by spending more time with friends. I could meet folks for coffee and hear their stories and be the kind of person who is caring and interested in their lives. But that takes time. Maybe if I watched less television or stopped listening to music. But I like music. Maybe I should take guitar lessons and try to get better. Perhaps practicing an hour a day would help . . .

Wait! This self-help thing is crap! There is no end to it. Even though there isn't a bad thing on the list and all of it could be helpful, I could end up wrecking my life. And would any of it ever result in joy? Probably not. Knowing me, I'd just end up resentful for having to drink those green shakes after walking five miles. There is nothing wrong with taking steps to improve ourselves, but the reality is we will never experience joy as the result of a self-improvement program.

Joy doesn't come from our frantic efforts to fix and improve ourselves. Rather, in the midst of real life, God wants to meet us and surprise us with joy in unexpected ways and at unexpected times. Even in hard, painful experiences, we can gratefully discover we are loved and valued. This love is ours even if we don't run around trying to fix ourselves. Jesus cares for us. He doesn't care about our schemes for self-improvement. I don't think he cares if I drink green shakes or not. Nor will he love me one bit more for drinking green shakes. Would he love me less if I stopped drinking them? I really don't think so. He wants his joy to be in us and our joy to be full. That is the best kind of self-improvement.

10

Discover Your Quest by Asking Questions

No, no! The adventures first, explanations take such a dreadful time.

Lewis Carroll

If you want to learn the art of asking questions from experts, simply observe four-year-old kids. On days when I volunteered as a helper in our preschool, I was impressed at the ability of these four-year-olds to ask questions. Even more impressive was that they did it with a naturalness and a candid innocence I rarely see in adults.

At first, their questions bugged me a little because I wasn't accustomed to such honest inquiry, about everything, all the time, seemingly without end. But after a while, it became apparent that asking questions is simply how they navigate their way through the world that is opening up all around them. I guess questions help kids the same way built-in radar helps bats navigate the darkness.

Studies show that our ability to ask questions is at its highest level when we are four or five years old. After that our questioning skills deteriorate with age and education, until we are so old and so educated that we no longer ask good questions. We don't lose the ability to question; we simply stop using it.

As we grow, we learn to stop questioning. We realize that teachers want answers, not questions. In school, we are taught how to find the right answers. College is an interesting exercise in learning how to present answers in a learned way. So after gaining way too much education, what chance do we have? Life is all about answers, answers, answers.

At work or in church, it is often considered weakness or possibly disloyalty to ask questions. Promotions and accolades usually go to those bright people who fired answers at every opportunity. So to fit in and prosper, we look for answers.

Like most of the adults in this world, I stopped asking questions and focused on giving answers. And I was pretty good at it. When someone came to me with a dilemma or a problem, I gave answers that were clear, rational, and I hoped helpful for whatever they faced. Thinking about those times, I'm amazed at how brash, swift, and overly confident my answers were. I must have become dumb, or at least dumber, as I've made my way through a labyrinth of heartache and unexpected challenges. My answers come a lot slower these days.

<hr/>

I'm impressed by knowledgeable people. Regardless of the topic, if someone knows stuff, I assume they are much smarter than I. My great-uncle King Hubbard was the smartest person I've ever known. Born and raised in the barren stretches of San Saba, Texas, he looked like any of my West Texas relatives at the family get-togethers. Though he didn't seem to have much to say, I grew up being told he was the smart one of the family. Turns out it was true.

King was a geologist who studied the oil-rich terrain of West Texas. He knew oil, math, and geology. Only when I grew older did I come to know that he had been simultaneously celebrated as a scholar and ridiculed as a fool. He was the first person to discover that with our known oil drilling capabilities, there would be a worldwide oil shortage of catastrophic proportions in the year 1972. Of course, he announced this in the mid-1940s, when most of his peers assumed he was crazy. They named his theory Hubbard's Pimple. I hope they lived long enough to be stuck in the long gas station lines we endured in 1972 at the height of the global oil crisis.

Uncle King knew stuff I will never be able to comprehend. But outside of his expertise, he was a pretty ordinary man. During all the years I knew him, I never heard him ask a single question. Perhaps he wasn't interested, or maybe he simply lacked social skills and couldn't engage in basic conversations. Fortunately, my aunt gracefully made conversation with everyone who came near.

Knowledge may come from seeking answers, but understanding can come from asking questions. Uncle King showed me that a person can have great knowledge and lack basic understanding.

Is it any wonder that we are focused on answers when so much of our status, success, and self-esteem depend on being right, or at least appearing right? When I meet with a couple seeking marriage counseling, it doesn't take very long for me to see how important it has become for one or both of them to be right. Sometimes they need to be right in the big issues and challenges, but just as likely this need shows up in the tiny, insignificant disagreements.

While having dinner at Bill and Jennifer's home, I casually asked how far they were from their son's school. Bill, reaching for the rolls, answered, "Oh, two miles." Jennifer immediately jumped in and said, "No, Bill, it's 2.3 miles!" I didn't want to get in the middle of that issue, so I asked him to please pass me the rolls.

Recently, while sitting in Starbucks (that's what we do in Seattle), I couldn't help eavesdropping on a conversation at a nearby table. A twentysomething man was discussing his favorite TV shows, and it was obvious that he was passionate about certain programs. He was explaining with enthusiasm the various subtleties of *Mystery Science Theater 3000* to an older man who might have been his uncle. I knew about *MST3000* because my son, Damian, had sat me down and forced me to watch these clever shows that feature robots watching B movies while making witty comments.

Even though the young man obviously knew the program inside and out, his uncle kept commenting about how he, too, knew a lot about *MST2000*. It wasn't long before they began to debate whether the name of the show was *MST3000* or *MST2000*. It took incredible self-control on my part not to turn around and yell, "It's *MST3000*! Let it go!"

Finally, the older man ended the argument by declaring, "It was originally called *MST2000*. They just recently changed the name to *MST3000*."

I sat and thought, "What was that all about?" Why were they willing to argue about something so trivial and miss a chance to share meaningfully and nurture a significant relationship? Then the realization hit me. I do the same thing all the time when I have to be right.

Observing this behavior in me, my friend Bruce Larson pointed out, "John, you have a choice to make. You can be right, or you can be well, but you can't be both. If you have to be right, you can't be healthy." I admit that stung a little. I even tried to come up with a response that would prove him wrong in this particular instance. Of course, my desire to be right about this only demonstrated how wrong I was.

<hr />

Whoever invented Trivial Pursuit was a genius. What better way to impress people at a party than to send the message, "See how smart I am and how dumb you are." Don't get me wrong. I love playing party games like Trivial Pursuit. It is amazing to watch people demonstrate their ability to recall the most meaningless facts on demand. Have you noticed that some people even have specialties to their knowledge of trivia? My friend Jim knows obscure baseball facts. I don't understand how he does it, but he can rattle off the name, position, and batting average of any player on any team in any year. My wife, Eileen, has the impressive ability to recall minutia about movies. Ask her who won the Oscar for best actress in 1947, then sit back and be impressed by her knowledge.

I grew tired of being the one who didn't know much when we played Trivial Pursuit. I'm not usually a quiet person, but I could have passed for a monk who had taken a vow of silence when the questions started to fly. I decided to fight back. So I picked a specialty and studied, memorized, and even practiced in front of the mirror so I would be ready with my quick answers should someone wander into my field of expertise. The subject never came up. Maybe my topic was too obscure. It is disheartening to know something that no one cares about. I was about to give up and admit I was a trivia loser.

Then my elderly parents called to invite us on a cruise to celebrate their sixtieth anniversary. It was a wonderful time for the entire family to be together and love on my parents. Then one night it happened: ship-wide trivia would be played on Thursday night. The showroom was packed, but the game was also broadcast into every cabin so all passengers could participate.

Naturally, I sat quietly as question after question was asked. I didn't know any answers and was feeling stupid, so I decided to walk out on the whole fiasco. But then, just as I was getting to my feet, the cruise director announced it was time for the final question. Whoever answered it correctly would receive the ultimate grand prize.

Only one more question. I sat down to wait it out. Then it happened! I couldn't believe my ears. Could they really be asking something I knew? The cruise director read the question one more time. "What was the name of the actor who played Tarzan in the very first Tarzan film? And what was his chest size?"

Many wrong answers were thrown around, including Johnny Weissmuller at least three times. Finally, I rose to my feet and waved to the cruise director, signaling I knew the answer. My heart was pounding in my chest, my hands were sweating profusely, and my throat was drying up to the point I might never swallow again, but I knew the answer. When he came over to me, I blurted out, "The first Tarzan was Elmo Lincoln, and he had a fifty-two-inch chest!"

I'm not sure what I was expecting as an audience response, but my answer wasn't met with thunderous applause or cheering encouragement. The room was mostly quiet with a few loud grumbles about it being an unfair question. Then the crowd started wandering off even while I anticipated receiving the grand prize. "What would it be?" I wondered. Probably free cruises for the rest of my life, or at least for the next year. Maybe a cash prize—that would be great too. It was a bit of a letdown when the cruise director finally handed me the prize: my own plastic model of the Carnival cruise ship. In that moment, I realized just giving answers alone is not enough; we need an inquiring mind and a caring heart.

When life starts to fall apart, I don't particularly like any of the answers people give me. Even well-intended advice seems too simple or not right for me. Maybe it will help others, but not me. As the hurt grows deep inside me and I am more frayed on the surface, I act like the guy taking a multiple-choice test. I choose "none of the above."

Instead of looking for more answers, my usual instinct is to start questioning. I question myself, my motives, my actions, and my abilities. Then I turn and start questioning everyone around me. If that isn't enough, I go straight to the top and have lots of questions for God to answer. In case you are wondering, I don't think God is bothered at all by our questions. Would a loving parent be perturbed when their child comes to them with a question? Of course not. Well, maybe if we are on a family vacation and the child keeps asking, "Are we there yet?" That might wear us down.

ıııııııııııııııııııııııııııı

Jesus frequently encountered men and women from various walks of life. Some reached out to him in crowds, others came to him privately, and some appeared in chance encounters he seemed to welcome. One question he frequently asked was, "What do you want me to do for you?"

We find Jesus engaged with people in two very different situations in Mark 10. The first involves two of his closest friends, who came to Jesus with a selfish request. "'Teacher,' they said, 'we want you to do for us whatever we ask.' 'What do you want me to do for you?' he asked. They replied, 'Let one of us sit at your right and the other at your left in your glory.' . . . When the ten heard about this, they became indignant with James and John" (vv. 35–37, 41).

Shortly after this encounter, we read, "As Jesus and his disciples, together with a large crowd, were leaving the city, a blind man, Bartimaeus . . . was sitting by the roadside begging. When he heard that it was Jesus of Nazareth, he began to shout, 'Jesus, Son of David, have mercy on me!' Many rebuked him and told him to be quiet, but he shouted all the more. . . . Jesus stopped and said, 'Call him.' So they called to the blind man, 'Cheer up! On your feet! He's calling you.' Throwing his cloak aside, he jumped to his feet and came to Jesus. 'What do you want me to do for you?' Jesus asked him. The blind man said, 'Rabbi, I want to see'" (vv. 46–51).

Why would Jesus ask a blind man, "What do you want me to do for you?" Isn't it all too obvious? What else would he want besides the ability to see? Jesus's response indicated he didn't presume or prejudge what the man desired. This openness allowed Bartimaeus to consider his options and ask for the thing he wanted most. He could just as well have asked for a special donation. A little something for his effort might have been all he sought. Because Jesus left the door open, Bartimaeus was free to ask for whatever he wanted, and in this case, Jesus responded to his request and healed his blindness.

How would you respond to Jesus's question, "What do you want me to do for you?" Take time to consider this carefully. The old saying "Be careful what you ask for" may apply here. James and John wanted to have priority and position over all the other disciples. I wonder if in the years that followed they regretted their selfish, stupid request. In response to Jesus's question, all they were able to come up with was priority on a seating chart. Really? That was the best they could do?

~~~~~~~~~~~~~~~~~~~~~~~~~~~~

Jesus asked great questions. In our modern culture, our emphasis on finding and giving answers keeps us from experiencing the power of asking questions. Questions can be powerful because asking a good question at the right time can open doors of understanding, opportunity, healing, and growth.

We discover new, fascinating things about people as they open up in response to our questions. When we ask questions, we are communicating that we are interested in people and want to hear from them. We are honoring the other person and sending the message that who they are and what they think matter to us. Successful salespeople understand the significance of asking questions that help clients determine what they need. The best therapists use appropriate questions to delve below the surface in order to address issues the person may not be aware of consciously.

Of course, not all questions are good questions. At a family reunion, the grandchildren were sitting around reminiscing about their various experiences with their grandpa. They burst out laughing when my nephew did an amazing imitation of Grandpa. "Do you want a spanking?" They all chimed in, "Yes, we do, Grandpa!"

Some questions are intended to belittle and undermine us. "What makes you think you are capable of doing this job?" "Why would we trust you now when you let us down in the past?" Of course, there are the parental classics, "Do you have a brain in your head?" and "Close the door. Were you born in a barn?" Never having visited a farm, I didn't understand whether the barn door was supposed to be open or closed, so it made no sense to me. Maybe I should have asked them why they didn't know where I was born, but then they would have asked me if I wanted a spanking!

When we are getting to know a person, good questions asked in timely ways help us open up and build trust with each other. We can start with questions that are nonthreatening such as those about personal history: Where did you grow up? Did you have a large or small family? What did you want to be when you grew up?

After asking and sharing about our histories, we can broaden our questions to include the present. Asking about where they live, work, and play helps us gain an understanding of the current terrain of their life. Everyone has a context in which they live and grow. Though we don't often pay attention or even notice it, our environment affects our perceptions and experiences.

My brother Richard is developing vineyards east of San Diego. I thought he was a little crazy when he bought several parcels of rugged land, dug wells, and began planting grape-vines. It wasn't long before I'd go down to visit and end up spending time in the vineyards, learning more about farming than I ever thought possible. He is teaching me about terroir, which relates to how the growing conditions such as climate, location, water, soil condition, and even pruning techniques all contribute to the quality of fruit that is produced. Dirt evidently isn't all the same. The condition and makeup of the soil significantly impact the quality and flavors of the grapes.

When I pointed out that some acres looked rough and rocky, with steep slopes in places, he explained that some of the best wine comes from the most rugged ground. Evidently, when vines struggle to grow and produce in less than perfect conditions, the fruit develops a complexity of flavor that is superior to that of fruit grown in seemingly stress-free environments.

I began to wonder if the terroir principle applies not only to vines but also to people. We see men and women every day who seem to rise above the difficulties and stresses they grew up in. Like many of the vines growing in Westfall Vineyards, they seem to embody strength of character in spite of their surroundings. Perhaps the more we understand our various settings, the more we can appreciate our unique qualities that show our true character.

After we have asked questions related to personal history and current settings, we can seek out their ideas, opinions, and viewpoints. The questions that are helpful to ask are those that communicate, "I want you to share your wisdom." When we invite someone to share their ideas, which flow from their experiences and history, we are honoring them and letting them know we hear them. Too often when this step is left out, people feel used and exploited.

Once when I was leading a fund-raising effort for a church building campaign, Bruce Larson advised me, "Don't pick their pockets without first picking their brains." He went on to explain how people will support what they help to create, so if they feel listened to, if their ideas are considered, and if they are taken seriously, they will give generously. If, however, people sense we want only their money and not their input, they might donate a little, but they won't give joyfully.

Some people were raised with the message, "No one wants to hear from you." Believing that their opinions and ideas are worthless and maybe even stupid, they've grown accustomed to letting others do the talking. We need them to share, for our benefit as well as theirs. When I notice someone sitting on the sidelines during a lively conversation, I ask them to share their thoughts on the subject, and after some initial embarrassment, they often bring the most important ideas to the discussion. A few questions can draw a person from the shadows into the light of honest communication simply because we asked for their wisdom.

After we've asked questions about personal history, current situations, and opinions, we have a foundation built on the blocks of mutual listening, caring, and valuing. Now we can approach those questions that open the door to deeper intimacy. One of the most helpful words to use in framing our questions is *how.* "How do you feel when . . . ?" "How do you handle . . . ?" "How do you want . . . ?" "How can we help with . . . ?" "How do you hope . . . ?"

There were times when someone shared some of the things they were feeling, and although I wanted to be helpful, I responded in ways that hindered the communication rather than helping it. Sometimes I jumped in with solutions to a problem or advice for the person to follow. Other times I froze, not knowing what to say, though my silence may have seemed like indifference or disapproval. Of course, the times I most regret are those when someone shared their feelings, and I reacted so forcefully that it seemed my response was going to overpower the feelings they had expressed to me.

I'm grateful for lots of grace and the many chances I've had to grow as a friend and a listener. Now when people share their feelings, I ask them, "Is there something you want me to say?" Or "Is there something you want me to do?" Sometimes they say yes and suggest things that might be helpful for me to say or do. Other times they respond no and remind me that my listening is fine. Since I am not very good when it comes to being a mind reader, I'm relieved of the pressure to try to guess what they might need or want from me. When we sincerely ask what someone needs, the other person is empowered to decide for themselves what they may or may not find helpful.

⸻

Sometimes we misunderstand what is being asked, or are unclear how to answer a question. A woman called to get information about our church. She was thinking about visiting on Sunday but didn't even know where we were located. I answered many questions about the church's style, attitudes, and beliefs. Then she asked, "Where are you at?"

I paused for a second and answered, "Well, I'm dealing with a few issues in our family and with my ADHD. I sometimes have trouble focusing, but overall I'm doing good."

"No, I meant where are you located. I need directions to find the church."

I started to give directions and asked, "Where are you coming from?"

She answered, "Right now I'm a single parent with two little kids. I'm working as a server in a restaurant, but I really want to finish school and go into nursing someday."

Laughing, I said, "I just meant which direction would you be driving, north or south."

||||||||||||||||||||||||||||

How we ask a question is important if we are going to understand not just how to solve a current struggle but also the bigger picture of who we are and who we are becoming. It's not always easy to ask the right questions. Perhaps when we were growing up, our teachers were wrong when they said, "There are no dumb questions." Of course there are! I know because I've asked a lot of them over the years. We need to discover how to ask the right questions.

Throughout the Bible are examples of smart people asking dumb questions. We've already considered James and John. Have you ever thought about what you might ask Jesus if you were to meet him face-to-face? I hope our questions are better than the one the brothers asked. "Can one of us sit at your right and the other on your left when you come into your kingdom?" That one irritated the other disciples.

Instead of exploring bad examples or making a list of things we would like God to explain to us when we get to heaven, we might find it more helpful to consider the questions God asked people in the Bible. Those questions show us what God wants to know and also bring up some significant issues for us to consider. If we take God's questions seriously, they might not only help us understand ourselves better but also help us move forward on our adventure with greater freedom and courage.

The first question God asks in the Bible is "Where are you?" (Gen. 3:9). When the first man and woman felt afraid, they hid from God, but he came looking for them. Since earliest times we humans have been hiding, concealing, and covering up as ways to keep others from knowing the truth about us. When God asks, "Where are you?" he doesn't ask because he doesn't know. He's giving us an opportunity to stop hiding and start living in his presence without pretense or defensiveness.

After Cain kills his brother, God asks, "Where is your brother?" Cain responds, "I don't know," then adds a familiar question of his own: "Am I my brother's keeper?" (Gen. 4:9). God's question to Cain helps us realize that we are not meant to live selfishly and disconnected from others. Our brothers and sisters may be from our families of origin, but they are just as likely to come from our relationships of choice: these are the relationships we choose to enter, which enrich our lives, and in which we discover how to love and care for others. Of course, there are even broader connections that are equally significant. Our place in God's family and even the human family bids us consider, "Where is your brother?"

Elijah was a person just like us, the Bible reminds us (James 5:17). At first glance, I didn't see the similarities. Reading about him in the Bible, I saw that he was bigger than life as he trusted God and brashly challenged the leadership and culture of his day. Yet other times he was fearful, ran for his life, and was depressed and bitter. On second thought, he was like us after all. God's question to Elijah, "What are you doing here?" (1 Kings 19:9) needed to be asked more than once.

"Who do you say I am?" Jesus asks his closest friends (Matt. 16:15). The world is full of opinions and perspectives about who Jesus is. A good man, a wise teacher, a religious prophet, a crackpot, a revolutionary, a misguided do-gooder, or as Peter answered, "You are the Messiah, the Son of the living God" (Matt. 16:16). This question cuts through all speculation and goes straight to the heart of the matter. It is a question for each of us to seriously consider and honestly answer.

On the first Easter morning, Mary stands outside the empty tomb weeping. Turning, she sees Jesus standing there but at first doesn't realize it is him. He asks, "Why are you crying?" (John 20:15). This question invites us to consider our heartaches, losses, and deep hurts without embarrassment or shame. Tears were God's idea. Why else would he make us with tear ducts and a great capacity for love and the emotions that accompany it? Jesus's question allows us to explore our feelings and to understand that we may have different reasons for our tears. There are tears of anger as well as tears of joy. Crying can be a means of manipulation or perhaps a way to control other people. It often is a healthy way for our bodies to release pent-up emotions and frustrations. When we allow ourselves to consider, "Why are you crying?" we take an important step toward wholeness.

Peter and Judas had both betrayed Jesus. One committed suicide, and the other went home and returned to the life he had known before meeting Jesus. In the days following the resurrection, the Bible tells us that Jesus went to Peter, found him working at his old job in the family fishing business, and asked him, "Do you love me?" (John 21:15). There will be times when we totally blow it. We will let down those we love, we may turn away from our faith, we may fall in a grand, humiliating fashion. Perhaps, like Jonah, we may know clearly what God wants from us yet choose to run the opposite direction. When we do the worst, where is God? Does he leave us in misery and shame? Does he give up on us and go after people who are more worthy? No. He is still with us, even at our worst, and he asks us, as he asked Peter, "Do you love me?"

The questions God asks show us that God not only knows us intimately and understands our struggles but also wants us to make choices that lead us to a full and healthy life. For a homework assignment, I invite you to write down each question, then begin exploring your own responses.

1. Where are you?
2. Where is your brother?
3. What are you doing here?
4. Who do you say I am?
5. Why are you crying?
6. Do you love me?

These questions shine a light to help us see who God is and how God relates to us. They also raise important issues for us to consider about life and how it can be lived. They are invitations to connect with God in a deeply personal way. These questions may bring to mind questions you'd like to ask God. Keep in mind he is not intimidated by our questions. I believe he welcomes them because they are building blocks for a relationship that will change us forever.

11

All We Need to Know
Is All We Need

I am with you always.

Jesus

A few years ago I was waiting in the Spokane airport for a Southwest Airlines flight. Sitting next to me was a man whose fashion style could be described as well-worn. His face and body looked like ten miles of bad road. I was trying to appear busy hoping he wouldn't start a conversation. Suddenly, he leaned over and asked what I did for a living.

When I'm traveling, if I want to engage with people and have conversations, I answer the question by telling them I'm an author. This is usually mildly interesting to people and opens the door to some great conversations. But if I want to be left alone, I tell them what I told the man next to me. "I'm a pastor!" That usually ends any dialogue and leaves me in peace and quiet for the remainder of the flight. But instead of pulling away, he leaned closer and said, "I'm in the same line of work as you." I tried not to show my disbelief, but I was curious enough to ask, "Oh, are you a pastor too?"

"No, not a pastor. I raise sheep; got a ranch just outside of town. I bet if you came and worked on my ranch for one summer, I could teach you all you need to know about pastoring a church." Well, I thought that was a little bold and perhaps there was a little arrogance sprinkled in for good measure. But just then my flight was called, so I excused myself and quickly scooted away to board the plane.

Sitting in my aisle seat near the front, I saw the stranger enter the plane and start down the aisle. When he saw me, he grinned and said, "What a lucky day. I'm in the middle seat right next to you!" *Oh, lucky me*, I thought.

He asked me if I knew anything about sheep, to which I responded, "Just the three s's: they are stupid, stubborn, and smelly!" Instead of laughing hysterically at my obvious wit and cleverness, he kind of stared at me like I was the dumbest thing he'd seen in a while. For the next several hours, my "friend" shared way more about sheep ranching than I ever would want to know. He shared a lifetime of learning about how sheep are fed, led, nourished, and nurtured. More than once since then I've thought of visiting his ranch in order to learn how to be a better pastor.

⸻

Moses ended up watching sheep. It wasn't his first career choice after growing up in the most powerful family the world knew at that time. The adopted son of Pharaoh's daughter, he was instructed, empowered, and prepared to accomplish great things. Then everything went wrong. In a fit of rage, he murdered an Egyptian and tried to cover up his crime by hiding the body in the sand.

Evidently, he wasn't that good at covering up, because the next day he was confronted by people who knew what he had done. When Pharaoh learned that his adopted grandson had murdered an Egyptian, he planned to kill Moses. Disconnected from his birth family, alienated from his adopted family in the palace, and distrusted by the Hebrew people, Moses fled into the wilderness, where he would live in exile, marry, and raise a family while working for his father-in-law herding sheep.

His days in the desert with the sheep were not necessarily bad, but they were very different from his previous life in Egypt. Everything had gone wrong, and he had lost any semblance of how things used to be. I'm pretty sure he had no idea that the adventure was about to begin as he led the sheep up the remote hillside and noticed a bush that was on fire.

At the burning bush, God called him by name (Exod. 3:4). The very idea that the God who made the universe and everything in it knows us and calls us by name is astounding. He isn't impersonal or aloof. On the contrary, God is involved and not indifferent. Moses answered right away, "Here I am" (Exod. 3:4). But in a short time, he would go from "Here I am" to "Who am I?"

The encounter shows how specific and engaged God is. "I have indeed seen the misery of my people in Egypt. I have heard them crying out because of their slave drivers, and I am concerned about their suffering. So I have come down to rescue them from the hand of the Egyptians and to bring them up out of that land into a good and spacious land" (Exod. 3:7–8).

I can imagine that as Moses was hearing this extraordinary message he grew excited to learn that God was paying attention. God saw, heard, cared, and would rescue the nation of slaves. Just hearing that God was going to act on their behalf must have set his heart pounding. Perhaps he thought of his birth mother, who loved him so much that she sent him down the river in a basket to give him a future and a hope, which she couldn't provide.

"And now the cry of the Israelites has reached me, and I have seen the way the Egyptians are oppressing them. So now, go. I am sending you to Pharaoh to bring my people the Israelites out of Egypt" (Exod. 3:9–10).

I think Moses was hearing this good news and was feeling as if he might explode with exhilarating joy—that is, right up to the point it suddenly became very personal. When he heard the words, "So now, go. I am sending you," I can picture the entire conversation suddenly skidding to a stop.

Moses's initial response, when he first had heard God call him by name, was, "Here I am." Yet how quickly his attitude changed when he heard that he was the one God was sending to accomplish this miracle. "But Moses said to God, 'Who am I?'" (Exod. 3:11).

This is the first of five responses Moses used in attempting to get out of doing this new assignment. I'm intrigued by God's response to each excuse, because we discover everything we need to know as we head out on our own new adventure.

Moses raised a good issue by asking, "Who am I that I should go to Pharaoh and bring the Israelites out of Egypt?"

(Exod. 3:11). Notice that God didn't bother to answer his question directly. Rather, he answered, "I will be with you" (Exod. 3:12). It seems to me this would have been a great time for the Lord to clarify things by giving Moses a clear answer to his question. It's not like there wasn't an answer that would have satisfied. He could have said, "Good question. Allow me to point out some of your personal traits and experiences that uniquely qualify you for this mind-boggling task.

"First of all, you are a Hebrew by birth. You were also raised in the palace as Pharaoh's grandson. You had the finest education, leadership training, and opportunities. You probably still have important connections from your palace years.

"Of course, there was that murder you committed and tried to cover up. It got you in trouble and you fled into the wilderness, where you've lived in exile. But while there, you got a job working for your father-in-law. You learned about life in the wilderness and the Bedouin way of living. You have become adept at herding and caring for flocks of sheep. Everyone knows they are stubborn and willful and go every which way, not unlike the way many people behave. So now do you see why I have chosen you for this assignment?"

That might have been a pretty good response to Moses's question, "Who am I?" Rather than focus on Moses's unique abilities and rich experiences, however, God responded simply, "I'll be with you." Evidently, this was all he needed to know.

Think about your own background, upbringing, successes, and failures that brought you to this time and place. Consider preparing your own résumé for life: what is it that qualifies you or gives you a sense of competency, self-esteem, or value? Where have you been and what have you done that points to your ability to accomplish whatever you set your mind to?

Nothing about us qualifies us for the adventure that awaits us other than the reality that the Lord is with us. Beyond the presence of God working in and through us, there isn't much for us to feel confident about.

Compared to me, some of my friends seem like spiritual giants. They pray, study, serve, and live in ways that astound me. They can tell stories of seeing miracles, lives being changed, and people growing, but even those things don't matter very much. All of our experience, training, preparation, and personal strength doesn't matter. All we need to know is who is with us. God's presence, power, wisdom, protection, care, and guidance ultimately determine the value and effectiveness of our lives.

Moses's second response was basically, "Who are you?" Being careful not to commit, he framed the question hypothetically: "Suppose I go to the Israelites . . . and they ask me, 'What is his name?' Then what shall I tell them?" (Exod. 3:13).

God answered, "I AM WHO I AM. This is what you are to say to the Israelites: 'I AM has sent me to you'" (Exod. 3:14). Then, clarifying his identity, "God also said to Moses, 'Say to the Israelites, "The LORD, the God of your fathers—the God of Abraham, the God of Isaac and the God of Jacob—has sent me to you"'" (Exod. 3:15).

By now you'd think Moses's resistance would have begun to ebb. After all, he had been assured that God would be with him, and he had been given a name and a context so that the people would trust him. Moses should have been ready to go. Not quite.

"What about them?" This third question goes to the heart of our insecurity and worry about peer pressure. "What if they do not believe me or listen to me and say, 'The LORD did not appear to you'?" (Exod. 4:1). After all this time, very little has changed. Like Moses, we often worry what others will say or what they will think of us.

This time the Lord changed tactics and put Moses through exercises that served as signs to demonstrate God's power in Moses's life. Each of the signs involved potential disaster for Moses. First, he was told to throw his staff on the ground, where it turned into a snake. After initially running away from the snake, he picked it up by the tail as he was instructed. Even I know not to pick up snakes by the tail.

The second sign involved a dreaded, incurable disease. Moses was told to put his hand inside his cloak, and when he withdrew it, he was probably devastated to find his hand infected with leprosy. After returning his hand to the cloak, he drew it out to find it healed of leprosy.

Signs and wonders were God's response to Moses's concern about what others might do or say. Surely these would be sufficient to instill confidence in the reluctant sheep tender. But they weren't enough.

This time Moses used a physical disability as an excuse not to respond positively to the Lord. "Moses said to the LORD, '. . . I have never been eloquent, neither in the past nor since you have spoken to your servant. I am slow of speech and tongue'" (Exod. 4:10). Perhaps the dread of returning to his old home, Pharaoh's palace, where he had first started to stutter, felt overwhelming to him. Like so many people who live with disabilities, he may have been all too familiar with the stares, insensitive comments, and ridicule.

The Lord made a promise: "Now go; I will help you speak and will teach you what to say" (Exod. 4:12).

The message from God to Moses was consistent. I will be with you. Use my name as your credential and authority. My power will convince the unconvinced. And finally, I will help you live beyond your disability. What did Moses need? Exactly what God provided: his presence, relationship, power, and help whenever Moses felt inadequate. That is all we need as well.

After Moses died, Joshua became the leader to take the people into the Promised Land. God's promise to Joshua was this: "As I was with Moses, so I will be with you; I will never leave you nor forsake you" (Josh. 1:5). Joshua was about to face unimaginable challenges. God's response? "Be strong and courageous. Do not be afraid; do not be discouraged, for the LORD your God will be with you wherever you go" (Josh. 1:9).

꜏꜏꜏꜏꜏꜏꜏꜏꜏꜏꜏꜏꜏꜏꜏

I wonder if we ever get to the point where we know enough, are skilled enough, or are prepared enough to live on our own terms. I'm an advocate of lifelong learning, but I don't think the goal is to finally arrive at the place where we no longer need the abiding presence of the Lord in our lives. All we need is to know the Lord is with us through it all.

I know from experience that when we face painful difficulties, wondering if we have the strength to take another step, we must hold on to God's promise, "I will never leave you nor forsake you" (Josh. 1:5). This isn't a guarantee for pain-free lives, rather we need his abiding presence precisely because, as Jesus reminded his followers, "In this world you will have trouble" (John 16:33).

We all spend plenty of time planning our days, trying to prepare ourselves for whatever may come. In the process, insecurities bubble up as we wonder if we've made a mistake or perhaps left out something important from our plan.

It is easy to forget that we aren't alone. "'I know the plans I have for you,' declares the LORD, 'plans to prosper you and not to harm you, plans to give you hope and a future'" (Jer. 29:11). This may be all we need to know. God is at our side, and he has plans for us that are good. His intention is not to harm us but to give us a future and a hope.

If God's bottom line is to give me hope and a future, then God and I are definitely on the same page. All I need to know is that God isn't finished with me yet, and I can relax into his love and care. I don't need to get his attention, or try to prove my worth, or concoct plans and schemes to make life work a little smoother. What I need is to let myself be loved, see myself through the perspective of his tender mercy, and walk gratefully into the future that is already prepared for me.

Trusting that God's plans for me are good and that my future is secure in his loving care leads me to wonder about all the energy and effort I have squandered in my past. Do I have the courage to let certain things fall away with every step I take on my adventure? I wonder what I would need to let go of. Here is my list:

1. Disappointments I've carried around for a very long time
2. Resentments for small and great offenses I've endured

3. Defensiveness to shield me from real and imagined insults

4. Trophies to my failures that keep me mindful of my limitations

5. Trophies to my successes that remind me I used to be someone

6. My need to be right, strong, smart, good, and fun so people will love me

7. Anger and frustration, fear and loathing whenever the world doesn't go my way

There are more, I'm sure, but I already sense my life lightening up. I wonder what I'm going to do with all the time and energy I will have if I'm not dealing with those pressing burdens. Well, I'm not going to worry about that right now. Instead, I think I'll start focusing on the things for which I'm thankful. That won't be too difficult. There is so much, now that I think about it.

12

New Beginnings Are Possible and Necessary

> Change only scares the small-minded. The small-minded and me.
>
> Casey Affleck

As I was standing by the donut table at church one Sunday morning, a couple came straight toward me and asked, "Can people change?" I tried to swallow the bite of maple bar I had just bitten into, but it stuck in my throat, so I signaled for them to wait while I drank some coffee to wash it down. That little delay was just enough time for me to come up with a way to sidestep whatever difficulties were sure to befall me no matter how I answered their pointed question. In a flash of brilliant cowardice, I pushed the question back on them. "What do you think? Can people change?" Without hesitation, they blurted out their opposing convictions. He said yes and she said no at the exact same time.

I decided to take an informal and unscientific poll by asking people wherever I went that week if they thought people could change. I wasn't surprised to find a variety of differing opinions. Even in our own home, we didn't agree. Eileen had a quick and adamant yes, followed by one of those glances informing me of her unquestioning rightness. Damian said, "Of course people can change. If we can't change, I would be in despair!" Then he added, "Unfortunately, most people aren't willing to do the work, so they miss out on changes that are possible."

Because I tend to lean toward enthusiastic pessimism, I don't hold my breath waiting for people to change. I'm quick to assume that rather than changing, we just become more of what we always were. Crabby teenagers grow to be crabbier senior citizens, and kind grandmothers started out as kind moms. But I hope I am wrong. The reason I want to be wrong is very personal and has nothing to do with others. I hope that I can change.

What kind of adventure would our lives be if we couldn't move forward when everything goes wrong? Of course, doing so is difficult, and sometimes we feel like giving up, but we keep on going. New adventures, new relationships, and new dreams emerge with every step forward. Our lives may change and sometimes look very different, but they will always be our lives, and we will come through with grace and renewed strength.

llllllllllllllllllllllllll

A new bakery/café opened near where I live. The owner, Judy Schneider-Wallace, spent two years remodeling a 1920s cottage that sits on a hillside overlooking the ferry terminal on Puget Sound. She is new in the restaurant business. She's a former elementary school teacher turned baker with two kids.

When asked by a writer for the *Everett Herald* why she decided to get into baking, she replied that on one day in early September, "my life and the lives of my children changed in an instant." It was the first day of school. Her son was starting seventh grade, and her daughter was having her first day of first grade.

She described how it was a normal start of the school year for her as a teacher with a new group of second graders excited for school. Her husband, Paul, had volunteered in her classroom as usual for a few hours that morning.

"The day ended and I walked my class out to the buses and made sure each of my students were on their way home. Then I noticed that my daughter wasn't picked up. That was strange: Paul was supposed to get her. From that moment I knew something was wrong.

"That day, after Paul left the school, he had gone home and ended his ongoing battle with depression by killing himself. I was instantly a widow raising two children on my own."

She described how she tried to start creating a new life for herself and her children. The kids went back to school after the funeral, but she struggled with all the aspects of being a young widow. She and the kids went to support groups and doctors, and they moved into a new apartment. Eventually, she returned to the classroom and continued teaching, but she knew she needed to make some changes.

She spoke of taking time off from teaching in order to focus on her kids and rebuild her life. Eventually, she met a man whom she married and assumed life could get back to normal. "I thought my life as a teacher, something that I had done for twenty years, would continue on. I met my new class and was absolutely thrilled with the third graders who walked through my doors.

"After about a month of teaching I just wasn't myself. I had developed anxiety and panic attacks. This was not good for everyone and I let my principal know that I would need to take a medical retirement.

"I was devastated about not teaching. Now I had to figure out how to live a purposeful life while being a wife and mother. It was a hard time, but I have always been a fighter. How could I wake up in the morning, get my kids to school and then find joy and contentment?"

Judy enrolled in a local community college and took baking classes. She earned a baking certificate and began to dream about the possibility of combining her baking skills with her love for entertaining. Step-by-step the idea of her own bakery/café took shape. Now, sitting and looking out on the water, she says, "I may have hit the perfect niche. Plus, baking has always brought me joy."[1]

Judy's experience with beginning anew as a single mom following the tragic loss of her husband inspired me. I considered my own experiences and began to list some of the things we can do to help us begin again.

1. Accept change.

It isn't always easy for me to accept that things change, but doing so is necessary. Not just circumstances change. We also change. We may not feel the same way we used to, or have the same goals, or think the same way we did before.

We must resist the urge to resist accepting change and accept who we are, even as we honor who we used to be.

2. Focus on what matters.

Sometimes we waste energy and time solving the wrong problems. We can get distracted by lesser issues that surface periodically. When I'm in a stormy situation and there are many demands on my attention, I try to look at things the way Noah might have handled problems on the ark. Certainly the mice had issues, but he first had to deal with the elephants on the ark. We need to stop chasing mice and solve our elephant problem first.

3. Change your mind first.

The first step toward positive change is to change our outlook. "Be transformed by the renewing of your mind" (Rom. 12:2). We need to think differently in order to live differently. The struggle is that deep down we love change and we hate change. Perhaps what we really desire is for everything to stay the same, but just get better. That's not going to happen.

4. Dream crazy big and act stupid small.

Big dreams can help us see beyond our current circumstances. We need big dreams to motivate us toward a new adventure. Maybe there is a little bit of Man of La Mancha in my heart, because I am always interested in dreaming the impossible dream. However, it is easy to feel overwhelmed when we face big actions. Such feelings can stop us in our tracks so that we never get beyond dreaming. If we start with small actions, we won't be overwhelmed at the start. Small habits turn into life-changers over time.

171

5. Honor every step.

There is something we can learn from every step we take. I assume my first steps as a toddler were not perfect. If they were like the rest of my life, I'm sure I spent a lot of time landing on my diaper. Evidently, I kept at it with encouragement from my parents. We need to be proud of how far we have come. Maybe we aren't where we want to be, but we are much better than we used to be.

6. Virus-protect your brain.

I hate it when my computer gets infected with a virus. All the systems bog down, sometimes the screen gets hijacked by bogus protection software, and the virus spreads until it infects every part of the hard drive. When that happens, I can't get the computer to turn on much less work the way it was intended.

I'm beginning to think that when everything goes wrong, stresses are unrelenting, and we have difficulty imagining a new and healthy life for ourselves, it is because our brains are infected with viruses just like my computer. We need to clean the debilitating thoughts from our minds so we can begin to function the way God meant us to when he made us. Then it might be helpful to install a mental and emotional virus protection so that we have a defense against those infectious thoughts that rise up and try to take over and stop us from moving forward and experiencing the adventure we desire. Whenever self-defeating thoughts begin to creep into our minds, we can picture them being identified, isolated, zapped, and removed in the same way computer viruses are destroyed by protection software.

7. Say good-bye.

Every beginning is linked to a necessary ending. Too often we miss the adventure that lies ahead because we don't let go of the past. Henry Cloud writes in *Necessary Endings*, "Endings are necessary, but the truth is we don't often do them well. Although we need them for good results to happen in life and for bad situations to be resolved, the reality is that most of us humans often avoid them or botch them."[2] Sometimes we need to end things in order to experience growth. Like plants need pruning and trimming to prepare them for the next season of growth and fruitfulness, we need to be trimmed of what is no longer helpful in order to gain new health.

8. Pay attention.

It is easy to get distracted and lose our way. Not paying attention has resulted in setbacks for many of us. Too many times, when I'm driving down the freeway, my mind wanders and without thinking I take an exit that has nothing to do with my destination. Sometimes it is an exit I used to take whenever I drove to a previous job. While not paying attention, I automatically went the wrong way. It is especially easy to become distracted when we are under stress. Staying in the present moment and paying attention help us to be our best self now.

A sixty-seven-year-old woman from Belgium learned the importance of paying attention when she followed (faulty) directions from her GPS. Sabine Moreau wanted to go only about ninety miles from her hometown in Belgium to pick up a friend at the Brussels train station. Instead, she drove about nine hundred miles to the south, through several countries, before she realized something was amiss. It's unclear if she entered the address incorrectly or if the GPS was faulty.

Regardless of who or what was at fault, she drove for two days, stopped twice for gas, slept on the side of the road, and even suffered a minor car accident along the way. She finally admitted that she wasn't paying attention. "I was distracted," she told *El Mundo*, "so I kept driving. I saw all kinds of traffic signs, first in French, then German and finally in Croatian, but I kept driving because I was distracted. Suddenly I appeared in Zagreb and I realized I wasn't in Belgium anymore."[3]

Problems like this one are relatively easy to fix. All that is required is for us to realize something is amiss, get off the highway, turn around, and drive back to Brussels. I wish all of our foibles could be remedied that easily. Perhaps they can. Think about how many of our problems could be corrected if we acknowledged the problem, stopped what we were doing, turned around, and went a new way.

〰〰〰〰〰〰〰〰

When it comes to change and new beginnings, expectations can be a wonderful blessing, or they can be a debilitating curse. I want people around me who expect me to do well, encourage me to do my best, and are not surprised when I have small victories along the way.

Of course, other expectations hold us back or remind us of things we don't need to be reminded of. Negative expectations can become a major obstacle keeping us from experiencing healthy change.

Over the course of life, expectations are formed in the minds of people about us, and in our minds about them, so that when we get together, it is easy to slip back into old patterns and behaviors without even thinking.

So many times I've gone to family get-togethers and I've immediately reverted back to acting like the thirteen-year-old boy I once was. It doesn't take very long before the severely middle-aged man I've become starts to fade away and I'm acting, behaving, and talking as I did when I was a kid growing up in my family. Old patterns emerge, as do petty resentments and unspoken jealousies. Sibling rivalries flare, and soon I'm confirming people's quiet suspicions that nothing has changed and I obviously never grew up. As I drive away, I'm sad that I missed another chance to show how much I have changed.

Sometimes we don't let people change. We don't have room in our hearts to accept changes in people around us. It is easier to keep relating to someone based on past experiences than to make the effort to see them in a new light and relate to them as the changed individual they've become.

In the early church, when Barnabus invited Paul to join him in the work in Antioch, the church had a conniption fit. They had clear memories of the days before Paul's dramatic conversion. They remembered him as Saul, a powerful man with authority and a desire to kill followers of Jesus, destroy their churches, and arrest their leaders. Now they wanted nothing to do with him. He was not to be trusted, and they felt unsafe. Although Barnabus used his own good reputation to protect Paul, it was difficult for Paul to engage with the churches he had sought to destroy.

People involved in recovery tell of their experiences with change. They have found that when the troubled person begins to change, cleans up from their addiction, and starts to relate differently to those around them, suddenly everyone is upset. Their family, friends, and co-workers act frustrated because the person is not behaving the way they used to. Now everyone will have to change. In a family, when one person changes, it affects everyone. If one person stops acting in their usual dysfunctional way, everyone else's dysfunction becomes apparent.

ΙΙΙΙΙΙΙΙΙΙΙΙΙΙΙΙΙΙΙΙΙΙΙΙΙΙΙ

When I talk with people who have experienced significant change in their life, they usually don't say it came from study or seminars or even from reading one of my (life-changing) books. Most change, they recall, came about after they went through painful and difficult experiences. Losing a job, ending an important relationship, the death of a loved one, surviving a major crisis or failure, or facing a debilitating illness can lead to catastrophic problems, but they also can and do lead to significant and healthy changes in a person's life.

When someone is facing great disruption or sadness, believe them when they tell you that life for them will never be the same. It won't. Too often we assume it will never be good, but although it will change, it can still be good. Just in a different way.

I knew that moving from California to Minneapolis would bring about changes. I expected as much. But when I suddenly lost the job that brought me to the Midwest, I felt traumatized. To me, it felt like more than simply a job loss. It also meant we would lose our home, our income, our church family, and many friendships. Our credit was eroded for years, and I lost my sense of self-confidence. I began to wonder if

I would ever work again and worried about our family surviving financially and emotionally. I felt betrayed by those I considered friends, which left me wondering if I would ever trust people again or allow them to get close to me.

Looking back on those painful years, I realize I didn't want a new beginning. I just wanted my old life back. But my old life was not coming back, and deep inside I knew I would have to begin again simply because I was running out of options. Experiencing failure on such a complete scale was new to me, and there were times I was tempted to give up.

In the middle of my downward spiral, Damian made me sit down and watch a DVD of the movie *The Edge*. It was one of his favorite movies, starring Anthony Hopkins, who described it as the most important film of his career. Not many people have seen *The Edge*, and though we had watched it before, I saw it with a different perspective this time. Hopkins plays a billionaire who goes on a wilderness trek in which everything goes wrong. Stranded in the remote wilderness after surviving a plane crash, he is hunted relentlessly by a bear who has already killed most of his companions. Finally, only Bob, played by Alec Baldwin, and he are left to fight for survival. Alec Baldwin's character has lost the will to go on and is surrendering to the inevitable hopelessness of their situation.

"Why do men die in the woods, Bob? They die of shame!" Hopkins's character then goes on to describe some of the accusing questions we keep repeating inside our minds. How did I let myself get into this mess? Why wasn't I more prepared? Why did I let this happen? Why wasn't I more responsible? How can I face the people I have let down back at home? In the woods, men die of shame!

"What are you going to do, Bob? Lay down and die? Not me. I'm going to find a way to walk out of these woods. What about you, Bob?"[4]

Sitting in the late afternoon sun watching the movie, I realized I had a choice to make: change or be smothered in shame.

Looking back on that experience, I realize how little I understood of the significance that simply deciding to change would have on my life. Yet little by little, choice by choice, change by change, I began walking out of the woods alive and well. My life is different, and it's good. Healing for me wasn't easy or painless, but it was real.

||||||||||||||||||||||||||||||

Sometimes when we have experienced more than our share of abuse, pain, or feeling unloved, we start to believe that life can never change. The pain becomes a part of who we are, and not being loved is just the air we breathe. When we see ourselves as unlovable or resign ourselves to abuse, we start to assume this is simply who we are. Even when friends attempt to come alongside us in caring and loving ways, their efforts are rejected because all the hurt and pain has left us unable to receive love or even hear a new message of kindness.

"Shame is a deep, debilitating emotion, with complex roots," writes Dr. Angie Panos. "Its cousins are guilt, humiliation, demoralization, degradation and remorse. . . . Shame impairs the healing and recovery process causing victims of trauma to stay frozen, unable to forgive themselves for being in the wrong place at the wrong time. Shame leaves victims with feelings of sadness and pain at the core of their being."[5]

We could endlessly discuss which emotion is most destructive, and I'm pretty sure anger or fear would be at the

178

top of our list. But shame may be the most damaging because it distorts and ultimately destroys a person's image of themselves, causing them to believe they are deeply broken, worthless, inferior, and unlovable. Shame can evolve into hating ourselves and, if allowed to grow uninterrupted, can lead to self-destructive behaviors, self-criticism, self-blame, self-neglect, and sometimes suicide.

"While anyone can suffer from lingering shame," Beverly Engel writes in *Psychology Today*, "those who were abused in childhood tend to carry the most shame. Emotional, physical, and sexual child abuse can cause a victim to become so overwhelmed with shame that it can actually come to define the person and prevent her from reaching her full potential."[6]

Compassion is the antidote for shame. Self-compassion is a powerful means of countering the destructive messages shame inflicts on a person. Much has been written on the significant connection between shame and compassion, but recently there have been breakthrough studies at the University of Texas at Austin by social psychologist Kristin Neff. Neff has found that self-compassion can act as an antidote to the poison of self-criticism, which is a major aspect of intense shame.[7]

Healing our shame comes when we tell ourselves what is most needed: words of understanding and encouragement. When we take the time to demonstrate the same elements of compassion that reflect God's attitude and loving mercy toward us, we counter the critical, negative, condemning messages that pummel us in shame-based self-criticism.

Jane shared bits and pieces of her story, which involved painful abuse, years of feeling unloved and unworthy, and debilitating physical pain that now kept her almost completely immobilized. She had reached a painful depth of despair and self-hate and was inconsolable. We sat and talked in the front room of the old house where she lived alone with a cat she considered her only friend. I felt a little squeamish knowing that this house, where she had lived all of her life, was the place where so much abuse, heartbreak, and shame had been forced upon her.

Realizing how she rejected any attempts by people to show her love or simple kindness, I knew there was nothing I could say that would budge her from the deep pit of despair that had been dug over her lifetime. "I'm struggling not to kill myself," she mentioned casually, "because I don't want to abandon the cat. But if Bogey dies, I don't want to live another day."

When shame and hurt overwhelm us, they can become our entire identity. The horrendous message that we are alone and unloved blares so loudly that it blocks us from recognizing all the lovable, positive, and creative aspects of our lives. I knew Jane was a compassionate person and a gifted artist, helping thousands of hurting people as she worked as a therapist at a hospital crisis center. Her clients were in dire need and severe pain. She counseled victims of violent crimes, hopeless addicts, abused children, survivors of cancer, and survivors of attempted suicide. She volunteered at her church, assisting in various ministries, encouraging people in their faith. She seemed to have endless compassion for others.

Years earlier, our son, Damian, was about to start high school when he gave her the nickname Auntie Mame, the name of the outrageous character in the Broadway show of the same name. He thought she was the funniest, wisest, boldest, strongest, most creative person in the whole world. Even though we moved from Seattle to California, he stayed in touch with Auntie Mame. When problems overwhelmed him, relationships careened off course, or issues he didn't want to talk about with us dragged him down, he had someone who understood and cared for him.

Sometimes the sound of his voice would startle me awake in the night, and I'd hear him in the basement talking on the phone. During a particularly difficult period of time when he was struggling with depression and suicidal thoughts, he called her every night, and she always answered the phone. Whenever I probed about the late-night conversations, he would say, "Auntie Mame understands me." Her willingness to encourage him was significant in our lives. We'll never know for sure, but our son may be alive today because Jane cared enough to show compassion to a struggling boy who lived far away.

Nearly twenty years went by, and one Sunday morning, just before church was about to start, Damian burst into my office. "Guess what. Auntie Mame just walked in!" I hurried to meet her but didn't see the brash, bold, bigger-than-life person we used to know. There she was, but she was different. I went over and sat down next to her.

"I was planning to kill myself," she told me, "but I noticed a postcard in the mail telling about this new church starting up. When I saw your name as the pastor, I wondered if it was you, so I came to see." Her voice was barely a whisper, and the intensity was gone from her eyes. Every sentence communicated worthlessness, shame, loneliness, hopelessness, and never-ending pain. I was shocked and sad.

It is possible and perhaps even common to demonstrate compassion and kindness to those around us, even complete strangers, yet show no kindness to ourselves. Forgiveness may be readily extended to those who abused and crushed our spirits, while only self-hate is allowed to grow in our own hearts.

One afternoon we were talking, and I asked Jane how she was doing. She told me, "I'm having a weird inner conflict. On the one hand, I just want to die. Yet I'm facing major heart surgery and I'm afraid that I might die in surgery! What's wrong with me?"

We laughed nervously at that double-mindedness, then I asked if she was doing anything that might be giving her a reason (even a small one) to live. She began to tell me about a new habit she was practicing. "Every hour I stop and tell myself that I am loved by God whether I feel like it or not, and you know, I don't often feel it. I tell myself that I am not alone, that Jesus promised he would never leave me or forsake me. Then I tell myself to stop putting me down in my mind, and I remind myself that I am loved and forgiven. She started to smile and said, "I think I'm beginning to change."

"I'm tired of telling myself how worthless and unlovable I am. I want to live long enough to know I'm lovable." I wanted to cry when I heard her say this. We all should live long enough to know God loves us. Imagine how free our lives would be if we allowed ourselves to be loved regardless. It would change everything.

13

The Journey to the Center of You

Adventure is not outside man; it is within.

George Eliot

I was sitting with some kids at a pancake breakfast, and I asked my friend Madeline how it was going at school. She told me about her third-grade class and some of the projects she was working on. One of her homework assignments was to write about an animal of her choosing. She rolled her eyes and made an expression indicating she thought this was the dumbest assignment ever given to a third grader. I asked what she was going to do to make her story different from the others and more interesting.

"Well, the giraffe I picked is going to wake up one morning and have a terrible problem. His spots turned pink during the night. The rest of the paper will be about what happens next." I told her she was brilliant. She rolled her eyes again with a smile.

She was on to something. As a third grader, she figured out that life is about getting up in the morning, discovering the unexpected, realizing that things are not the way they ought to be or how we want them to be, and then figuring out what we're going to do about it. We may not wake up with pink spots, but we may find something else has gone terribly wrong. We are suddenly met with unwanted changes, emotional or financial turbulence, heartbreak and loss, or brokenness and betrayal. Although we don't want to deal with any of these troubles, the truth is that our struggle when something goes wrong gives our lives meaning and adventure.

Without impossible problems and terrible dangers, Superman would just be Clark Kent in all his boring dullness. Of course, sometimes I think it would be all right to have a life free from pain, grief, betrayal, and abuse. I might even daydream about how much easier life would be if I could just get away from it all.

There are times when we all would like to get away from our problems and concerns. What would that be like? I picture it like traveling across our great country with a group of very dull, problem-free vacationers in a glass-bottom tour bus. I can't think of anything more boring than riding through North Dakota looking down at the unchanging view through the glass floor of the bus. Of course, if we really want a trouble-free life, we should stay on the bus, and whatever we do, we shouldn't ask for adventure. This is as foolish as praying for patience, since patience comes from experiencing the terrible things we need patience to survive!

When I was a kid, the idea of going on a great adventure into an unknown world fascinated me. I wanted to be a daring explorer who ventured out and returned with treasures and discoveries that created shock and awe in my family and friends. Life didn't happen the way I was expecting. Instead, I read about adventures rather than experiencing them myself.

Having grown up in West Africa, I was drawn to the stories of Edgar Rice Burroughs and his Tarzan books. He wrote of strange, new worlds filled with wonder and fraught with danger. Then I read my way through the entire series of Nancy Drew mysteries, even though I had ridicule heaped on me for reading "girl books." (Who knows, maybe I've driven a little red sports car all these years because her boyfriend, Ned, had one.)

But one book stood out to me above the others, *Journey to the Center of the Earth* by Jules Verne. It was an epic story of a handful of people who traveled to Iceland and climbed down volcanic tubes to the center of the earth, which was pretty mind-blowing for a kid like me. Every time I saw a pile of rocks near our home, I hoped it was one of those secret entry points and that I'd have the adventure of my life. It always ended up being just a pile of rocks.

As I got older, I grabbed hold of any chance to kindle excitement by traveling to distant places where I'd meet strange people and eat weird food. But usually by the time I was headed home, the adrenaline rush would be wearing off, and I'd find myself slipping into depression and bogged down in boredom. Of course, I'd start scheming about the next trip I could take, hoping it might be a lasting adventure.

My friends tell me they will never go anywhere with me because too much stuff happens on a Westfallian holiday. Shortly after my mother-in-law died, I planned a little trip to Montreal. Eileen's mom, Lila, had been born there shortly before her parents returned home to Ireland. Since we'd never visited Montreal, I planned to take Eileen there in honor of her mother. I determined this was going to be the perfect trip.

My lack of planning has caused some problems in the past, so this time I carefully and meticulously made preparations for our vacation. First, I booked us on a cruise ship sailing from Quebec to Boston, with stops at various beautiful spots along the way. We were scheduled to fly from Seattle to Montreal, where I prepaid for deluxe hotel accommodations. After a perfect visit in Montreal, we would travel first class on the Canadian Railroad to Quebec, where I reserved a stay in a five-star hotel prior to our cruise departure. After the fabulous cruise, we were set to disembark in Boston, sightsee in that historic city, then fly home, having experienced the greatest, smoothest, most wonderful vacation ever. I couldn't wait to show how my careful planning and meticulous care would make this a memorable experience. What could possibly go wrong?

To eliminate any possible stress and guarantee a smooth departure, I took us to Sea-Tac Airport several hours before our flight. Something seemed wrong with the self-check-in machine, because it wouldn't print our boarding passes. No worries. I went in search of an airline representative who could clear up this little glitch and send us on our fabulous way. The first attendant couldn't make the machine work either, so she sent us to a help counter for assistance.

After waiting over an hour in line, we finally reached the counter and explained our problem. The clerk pecked computer keys for a while and then with a super-understanding, soft voice explained that boarding passes could not be issued because Eileen had only an enhanced driver's license and needed a passport to fly into Canada. I tried to explain that the enhanced driver's license was sufficient for Canadian travel, and I even pointed out that we had crossed the border many times by car, by foot, by boat, and by train. She pointed out that while that may be true, we wouldn't be going by airplane.

I shifted into problem-solving mode and worked with her to try to find a way for us to get to Montreal. First, we considered flying to New York City and catching a train from Grand Central Station to Montreal, but if we flew to New York, we wouldn't be in time to catch the last train. I came up with a workable alternative. We could wait at the airport for twelve hours, board a red-eye flight to Boston, and arrive early in the morning. Once there, we could rent a car, drive through morning rush-hour traffic, cross a couple of states, and cross the border to reach Montreal, where we could leave the rental car if we agreed to pay an exorbitant drop-off fee.

Our problem was solved, until the ticket agent said, "Sir, there is a problem." Because they wouldn't let us on our ticketed flight, even if we bought new tickets to Boston, they would automatically cancel our return tickets from Boston (since we had missed the first part of the round-trip ticket). Now I had to pay for new (way more expensive) tickets to Boston as well as buy (outrageously more expensive) tickets from Boston to replace the perfectly good ones they wouldn't let us use! Even reminding them that they were the "customer service" counter didn't help at all.

While we sat in the airport for the next twelve hours, I brooded about cosmic issues such as fairness, reasonableness, and inflexibility. My brooding didn't change a thing. Of course, our overnight flight was late, which pushed all our newly created plans into an impossible time frame, but by then I had given up any hope of having a perfect vacation.

We missed out on the first night at our prepaid hotel, but we at least got there for one night. Eileen sent me to get ice for our room, which seemed like a small request at the time. The ice machine on our floor wasn't working, so I went up to the floor above us and found that machine wasn't working either. Eventually, I climbed up and down the stairs until it dawned on me that every single ice machine in the five-star hotel was broken.

After carrying my little metal bucket to the reception desk, I was informed that the city of Montreal was having a little problem. Their water supply was polluted, so the water for drinking, making ice, and so on had been cut off. The clerk handed me two bottles of water, told me to be sure to use them for brushing our teeth, and suggested we ration them carefully. Ice was out of the question.

Tired from running up and down stairs and frustrated I had picked water pollution day for our visit, I walked down the street carrying my little bottles of water. Around the corner, men who looked a lot like characters in *The Sopranos* were hauling bags of ice into a darkened tavern. I had nothing to lose at this point, so I followed them into the shadowy lounge. They were kind enough to trade a handful of ice cubes for $20. I was starting to feel lucky once more.

The next morning at the train station, we were fortunate that the kind lady checking us in found several plastic bags for us to fill with the clothes that had to be removed from our suitcases, because evidently our bags were overweight for the train. I found it hard to maintain my dignity while sitting on the floor in a crowded depot shoving various personal items into little bags while knowledgeable Canadians stared at me, hoping and possibly praying they wouldn't have the misfortune of sitting near us on the train.

The cruise was uneventful, to our great relief. We disembarked in Boston, and as I had carefully planned, the taxi dropped us at a hotel right in the center of the old town. I had made arrangements to check our luggage at the hotel so we could enjoy the day exploring the historic town before flying home that evening.

The valets announced to us that the recent bombing tragedy at the Boston Marathon had resulted in a change of rules. Now they would not accept our bags. Explaining to the valets that Eileen was in a wheelchair following surgery on her spine didn't bring a speck of sympathy. Even I knew it would be impossible to push Eileen's wheelchair around the old cobblestone streets while attempting to haul overweight luggage in our wake. There was nothing we could do but sit in front of the hotel with all our bags and wait for nightfall so we could fly home. After a few hours, one of the valets felt sorry for us, and when no one was looking, he kindly agreed to take our luggage in exchange for a sizeable tip. It cost us a little less than what we might have spent to stay at the exclusive hotel.

Much later, we realized what an adventure our trip had been. It was nothing like we had planned, but looking back, we could say, "That was the best vacation ever!"

||||||||||||||||||||||||||||||

Why would we suppose that an inner journey would be different from a vacation? Realistically, the journey to the center of you may have even more frustrations, setbacks, and challenges. After all, we are embarking on a great adventure, and what we experience will be both personal and significant.

It is easy to try to create excitement and meaning through the pursuit of adventures that were "out there." Even the phrase "going on an adventure" conjures up ideas of heading out to some other place than where we are right now. But we may be missing out on the greatest adventure of all: the inner journey to the center of who we are.

Some people don't want to take this journey and avoid it by focusing on others. Sometimes if we are looking all around at other people's issues and lives, we can keep from having to look too closely at ourselves and what makes us tick.

When I am focused outwardly, my personal issues are limited to things such as where I might go and what I might do and who I might meet and what I might see, hear, or eat. I miss out on something much more significant, interesting, and fun. Why don't we jump at the chance to explore the world inside when we already know the world outside isn't going to be enough? We need to find out before we miss the greatest adventure of all—life.

When our grandchildren Zack and Ariel were quite young, we went on vacation in Southern California. They loved the swimming pool, but little Zack became frustrated because he didn't know how to swim. Rather than teach him to swim, I tried the quick-fix method: I bought him a set of water wings so he could stay afloat and not sink in the water.

Settling back on my lounge chair, I enjoyed watching him float around in the water, playing freely with other kids without the fear of sinking. After a while, Zack came over and sat beside me. "When I get home, I'm going to learn how to swim," he announced.

I tried to encourage him by telling him how great he was doing with the water wings, but his mind was made up. "Grandpa John, if I learn to swim, I could go deep down in the pool. With water wings, I just bob around on the surface." There was no arguing with that logic. Soon after we got home, Zack excitedly shared how he'd enrolled in swimming lessons and no longer needed water wings.

Maybe Zack was on to something. There have been so many times when I settled for an easy solution rather than doing the hard work that would make a difference. It's easy to put on emotional or spiritual water wings that will keep us bobbing along the surface of our lives and never experiencing the depths. Maybe we aren't in danger of sinking, but we also aren't experiencing what it is like to actually swim. If only we could be more like Zack and courageously remove the props that keep us on the surface so that we can live fearlessly.

When I look below the surface of my life, I can see that fear is something I've had with me for a long time. We can try to ignore it, pretend it isn't there, even cover it over with a hard shell of bravado, but fear seems to stay with us no matter what we do.

Jesus recognized fear in his closest friends. Sometimes he asked, "Why are you afraid?" Other times he simply pointed out that they were acting in fear and said, "Fear not!" He understands the weight of fear holding us down and keeping us from responding to his presence in our lives.

Getting below the surface of our lives can raise a lot of questions and trigger some basic insecurities. What will we find when we get there? What if we don't like who we are at the core of our being? What if there is nothing there? What if we find out the critical voices we've carried with us are right? What if we're not lovable as we've always suspected? Wouldn't it be better not to know the terrible truth and just stay safe and shallow for the time being?

Many of us carry messages of self-criticism as we go through life. These messages can influence and even shape our actions and reactions as well as the choices we make. A friend told me she works so hard to prove herself worthy at work yet feels like a failure in her marriage, parenting, and friendships. "I feel like there is an accusing voice in my head constantly telling me I don't measure up."

I asked her if she had any idea where these harsh criticisms came from or who might have said these things to her. Before I could even finish my question, she blurted out, "You mean my mother?" Even though her mom had been dead for many years, she still carried her accusing voice reminding her that she would never amount to anything good.

I encourage you to take the journey to the center of you. In fact, I am confident of what you will discover and that it will make all the difference. When we set aside our water wings to freely explore the deepest parts of ourselves, we will find that the Bible is right: we are loved. Not because of anything we have done, achieved, earned, figured out, or accomplished but solely because we are unique, unrepeatable miracles whom God made, knows, and calls by name.

When the discovery of this treasure of love takes hold, it changes us in radical ways. The first changes take place within, far away from the views and opinions of others. But they don't stay inside or invisible. When we start to believe we are loved, this belief can't help but affect our feelings, attitudes, behaviors, and experiences in life.

At first, it may seem strange that none of the positive changes we experience depend on our efforts or actions. I've spent much of my life trying to fix myself and others, even though I've been pretty mediocre at it and have not accomplished very much. Have you ever tried to bear down and force yourself to feel loved? Or have you worked diligently to try to experience joy? Life just doesn't work that way.

There is nothing we can do to persuade God to love us one bit more than he already does. When we realize we are loved, we see that all the old ways of handling life and dealing with people or problems are not just ineffective but completely wrong.

<hr>

Our home is on a little lane that is wide enough for only one car to slowly wind along Puget Sound. When we encounter someone driving the other way, it is a big deal to back up or pull over without accidently sliding off the cliff to the rocks below so that we can pass by each other.

I've grown to love our location because the beauty of the water, the view of Whidbey Island, and an occasional bald eagle in a tree make the seemingly constant rainy drizzle of Seattle a little more bearable. We also have a ringside seat for an amazing array of boats, ships, and kayaks passing back and forth in front of our house.

Huge tankers and cargo vessels bring to our waters all sorts of exotic stuff, I imagine. When the salmon are running, dozens of fishing boats swarm to our area hoping for a great catch. Kayakers paddle around, and the other day I saw a guy standing up on something, paddling with a long oar, while his faithful yellow lab sat quietly in the bow of the boat. Occasionally, I catch a glimpse of a nuclear submarine chugging along accompanied by an entourage of naval vessels. One of my favorite sights is the late-afternoon sailings of cruise ships heading off to adventures in Alaska, with unlimited dining and midnight chocolate buffets on board.

Between our house and the water's edge run the train tracks. Until I moved in, I had no idea how busy our nation's railroads can be. The realtor who sold us the place informed us that there would be three or four trains a day, but he assured us we'd soon get used to the sound and not notice them going by. That actually sounded kind of nice to me. Who wouldn't enjoy the occasional passing of a train? It turns out there are forty-three trains a day. Some carrying oil and coal are nearly one hundred cars long. I counted them. Of course, when I say "day," I mean day and night!

With all these adventurous possibilities parading in front of me, I admit sometimes I'm tempted to succumb to wanderlust and imagine how exciting it would be to hop a train or board a ship heading who knows where.

One morning at breakfast, I watched a tugboat hauling a barge piled high with containers on its way to Alaska. I started to wonder what it would be like aboard that tugboat heading up the Northwest Passage. First, I thought how different from my life it would be and how exciting it'd be just to be a part of the ship's crew. I daydreamed about myself at sea, free from having to deal with all my issues back home. Then reality kicked in, and I pictured myself on the cramped boat, breathing diesel fumes while endlessly watching the water go by.

I'm grateful that after all I've come through, my biggest adventure is very near. Jesus told us the kingdom of God is near. Experiencing God's presence and power in my life is meant to be a great adventure. It isn't a mystery to be solved or a distant destination to reach, and unlike in *Journey to the Center of the Earth*, I won't even have to go to Iceland and climb down a volcano.

When we realize that the plans God has for us are good, to give us hope and a future, we are free to climb as high as our dreams will take us and go as deep as our love desires. We may not know what happens next, but we can be confident because we are not traveling alone.

Always remember that you are a unique, unrepeatable miracle. Your life is a gift from God. Now let the adventure begin.

Notes

Chapter 2 We Are All in This Together

1. Kurt Vonnegut, BrainyQuotes.com.
2. Paul Schoenfeld, "Are Middle-Aged Men an Endangered Species?" *Everett Herald*, March 23, 2016, D4.
3. Chris Cuomo, "School Holds Assembly to Honor Waving Neighbor," Newday.blogs.CNN.com, February 19, 2014.

Chapter 3 I'm Not Stubborn, I Just Don't Want To

1. David Wells, *God in the Wasteland* (Grand Rapids: Eerdmans, 1995), 114.

Chapter 4 Hope Comes in Unexpected Ways

1. "Welcome to McDonald's, May WE Take Your Order?" Brandautopsy .com, July 18, 2004.
2. *The Replacements*, directed by Howard Deutch (Burbank, CA: Warner Bros, 2000).
3. Jeannette Nolen, "Learned Helplessness," *Encyclopaedia Britannica*, https://www.britannica.com/topic/learned-helplessness.
4. James Collins and Jerry Porras, *Built to Last: Successful Habits of Visionary Companies* (New York: HarperBusiness, 1994).
5. Elon Musk video interview, *Wall Street Journal*, April 22, 2011.
6. Jeff Bezos, "The King of E-Commerce," Entrepreneur.com, October 10, 2008.
7. https://www.google.com/about/company/.

8. John F. Westfall, *Getting Past What You'll Never Get Over* (Grand Rapids: Revell, 2012), 31.

9. Stephen Guise, *Mini Habits: Smaller Habits, Bigger Results* (Seattle: CreateSpace Publishing Platform, 2013), 13.

Chapter 5 Only One Thing Can Silence Fear

1. *Shadowlands*, directed by Richard Attenborough (Savoy Pictures, 1993).

2. Ibid.

3. Rollo May, *Love and Will* (New York: W.W. Norton & Co., 1969), 138.

Chapter 6 What We Leave Behind Makes a Difference

1. Frederick Buechner, *The Hungering Dark* (New York: HarperOne 1985).

Chapter 7 Between Safety and Risk, Always Take the Risk

1. Mark Zuckerberg, Brainyquotes.com.

2. Kay Koplovitz, interview with Natalie Pace, *Huffington Post*, Huffingtonpost.com, May 29, 2013.

3. Pamela Barnes, interview with Carrie Murphy, "CEO Pamela Barnes of Global Women's Health Nonprofit EngenderHealth Talks Career Changes and Taking Risks," TheGrindstone.com, June 28, 2013.

4. Sarah Chang, "How to Get Over Your Fear of Taking a Career Risk," TheMuse.com.

5. Julia Cameron, *It's Never Too Late to Begin Again* (New York: Tarcher-Perigee, 2016), 118.

6. Chesterton.org/a-thing-worth-doing.

7. Marc Chernoff, "10 Risks Happy People Take Each Day," Marcandangel.com.

Chapter 8 Giving People the Weapons That Can Hurt Us

1. John Powell, *Why Am I Afraid to Tell You Who I Am?* (Allen, TX: Argus Communications, 1969).

Chapter 9 Eat More Ice Cream and Fewer Beans

1. Bob Goff, Goodreads.com, August 12, 2016.

2. Kris Kristofferson, spoken in concert, Rheem Theater, Moraga, California, March 22, 1993.

3. Debbie Bryce, "Lunch Lady Loses Job Over Free Meal," IdahoStatesman.com, December 21, 2015.

Chapter 12 New Beginnings Are Possible and Necessary

1. Andrea Brown, "Leavened Joy," *Everett Herald*, July 5, 2016, B1.

2. Henry Cloud, *Necessary Endings: The Employees, Businesses, and Relationships That All of Us Have to Give Up in Order to Move Forward* (New York: HarperBusiness, 2011), 13.

3. Mike Krumboltz, "Woman Drives 900 Miles Out of Her Way after GPS Error," YahooNews.com, January 15, 2013.

4. *The Edge*, directed by Lee Tamahori (Hollywood: Art Linson Productions, 1997).

5. Angie Panos, "Healing from Shame Associated with Traumatic Events," Giftfromwithin.org, referenced May 7, 2016.

6. Beverly Engel, "How Compassion Can Heal Shame from Childhood," Psychologytoday.com, July 14, 2013.

7. Marina Krakovsky, "Self Compassion Fosters Mental Health," Scientific American.com, July 1, 2012.

John F. Westfall is founding pastor of Harbor Church in the Pacific Northwest. A former radio show host, an ordained pastor, an adjunct professor at Fuller Theological Seminary, and a popular retreat and conference speaker, John is the author of *Getting Past What You'll Never Get Over*. He lives in the Seattle area with his wife, Eileen.

Sometimes you just can't
pick yourself up and move on.
But even then, THERE IS HOPE.

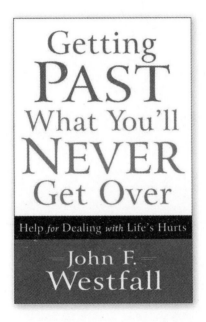

With deep compassion, John F. Westfall leads you
beyond your pain and into a life of confidence,
freedom, and secure joy. You may carry the wounds
of the past, but that doesn't need to keep you from
living a hope-filled future.